OXFORD TELEVISION STUDIES

General Editors **Charlotte Brunsdon**
John Caughie

Critical Ideas in Television Studies

Critical Ideas
in Television Studies

John Corner

Clarendon Press · Oxford
1999

Oxford University Press, Great Clarendon Street, Oxford OX2 6DP

Oxford New York

Athens Auckland Bangkok Bogotá Buenos Aires Calcutta
Cape Town Chennai Dar es Salaam Delhi Florence Hong Kong Istanbul
Karachi Kuala Lumpur Madrid Melbourne Mexico City Mumbai
Nairobi Paris São Paulo Singapore Taipei Tokyo Toronto Warsaw

and associated companies in
Berlin Ibadan

Oxford is a registered trade mark of Oxford University Press

Published in the United States
by Oxford University Press Inc., New York

British Library Cataloguing in Publication Data
Data available

Library of Congress Cataloging-in-Publication Data
Corner, John, 1943–
Critical ideas in television studies / John Corner.
(Oxford television studies)
Includes bibliographical references and index.
1. Television broadcasting—Social aspects. I. Title. II. Series.
PN1992.6 .C677 1998
302.23'45—ddc21 98–34735
ISBN 0–19–874221–5
ISBN 0–19–874220–7 (pbk.)

10 9 8 7 6 5 4 3 2 1

Typeset by Graphicraft Limited, Hong Kong
Printed in Great Britain
on acid-free paper by
Biddles Ltd.,
Guildford and King's Lynn

Oxford Television Studies

General Editors
Charlotte Brunsdon and **John Caughie**

OXFORD TELEVISION STUDIES offers international authors—both established and emerging—an opportunity to reflect on particular problems of history, theory, and criticism which are specific to television and which are central to its critical understanding. The perspective of the series will be international, while respecting the peculiarities of the national; it will be historical, without proposing simple histories; and it will be grounded in the analysis of programmes and genres. The series is intended to be foundational without being introductory or routine, facilitating clearly focused critical reflection and engaging a range of debates, topics, and approaches which will offer a basis for the development of television studies.

Acknowledgements

MY FIRST DEBT OF THANKS is to the editors of this Oxford series, Charlotte Brunsdon and John Caughie. Their detailed comments and suggestions on draft material helped me greatly both in the organization of the book and the development of its chapters. I would also like to acknowledge my immediate colleagues at Liverpool University, with whom I have discussed aspects of television over several years, sometimes in the course of working alongside them in teaching and research: Neil Gavin, Peter Goddard, Julia Hallam, Len Masterman, Kay Richardson, and Maggie Scammell. Conversations with a much broader range of colleagues at institutions both in Britain and abroad have shaped my thinking about themes and approaches in the study of television. Here, I would like to mention particularly my editorial colleagues on the journal *Media, Culture and Society* (Raymond Boyle, Nicholas Garnham, Anna Reading, Paddy Scannell, Philip Schlesinger, Colin Sparks, and Nancy Wood), Sylvia Harvey of Sheffield Hallam University, and Peter Dahlgren of the University of Lund, Sweden.

Mick Belson at Oxford has handled the progress of the manuscript with courtesy and promptness, for which I am very grateful.

J.C.

Contents

1

Introduction: Research and Criticism

THIS book looks at some of the ideas about television which have emerged in academic study. It does this through a sequence of ten short interconnected chapters, each one of which cuts into the protean character of the medium under headings indicating broad aspects of form and function. Just how any commentary such as this is divided into parts is, of course, a key feature of its intellectual design. My headings have a certain obviousness, going with the grain of current usage (e.g. institution, reception, production) but I have tried to use them flexibly. They are also, necessarily, neither fully comprehensive nor free of that lumping and splitting whereby things which for some purposes are best kept apart are put together and vice versa. At times, the connection is horizontal, with other ideas; at other times, it is vertical, either in the direction of particular substantive studies or of more general theoretical perspectives on media, culture, and society.

The treatment is mostly cross-generic and at a level of generality which precludes any proper synopsis of the dense academic literatures which have now grown up around many dimensions of television. There is a growing number of volumes which seek to carry out the latter task and, indeed, it is only by such specialist attention that a referencing of the full range of work can be anything other than indicative.

Although I hope it will be found accessible by students, and will stimulate their reading of the wider literature, it is not designed primarily as a textbook.

There are many aspects of television which are not touched on and even within the realm of ideas about it, although I have tried for a fairness of approach, I have worked from my own sense of the significant and the promising in ways which cannot be other than selective, occasionally partisan, and sometimes virtually autobiographical. My own career has involved working with both the social science and the humanities' approaches to television and my discussion attempts to make connections with both, giving particular emphasis to work which bridges the two. Some chapters (e.g. that on knowledge) can obviously achieve this more easily than others (e.g. that on narrative) which lean much more towards one than the other. In every chapter, I start my discussion by considering the relevant aspect of television itself and those questions about it which it would seem most useful to ask, introducing classifications and ideas of my own in the course of reviewing those of others. Often, I have made use of lists and typologies to improve the clarity of my exposition and to counter what I regard as a tendency in the field towards an inadequate differentiation between specific lines of argument and also between specific characteristics of television itself.

The extent to which I reach back into the history of debate about the medium varies with topic. It is clear, for instance, that attempts to gauge the impact of television upon public knowledge have been a feature of research and criticism since the very earliest studies, whilst interest in the distinctive character of television narrative or in the properties of broadcast speech is much more recent. The aim of reviewing ideas grouped around significant characteristics of television is to contribute to what I believe is a desirable phase of critique and consolidation in television research, following two decades of intensive activity in which some developments have lost touch with each other and, indeed, in some cases appear to have lost touch with television itself. Such a phase might not only help to make better sense of past and current arguments about television but it might aid in the construction of future criticism and research, which will need to follow television as the terms of its political and cultural identity shift.

Any attempt to offer sustained academic attention to television is beset by at least three problems right from the start. First of all, the various aspects of television as a process (economics, regulation, policy, production, programmes, audiences, influence, etc.) have produced their own radical division of labour in international scholarship, with a split between humanities and social science approaches very apparent. Secondly, generic interests (drama, news, documentary, comedy, etc.) have often pursued a mutually exclusive line of enquiry and intellectual debate. Thirdly, the linking of television with other aspects of culture and society (television and violence, television and the family, television and election campaigns, television and nationalism, television and narrative form, television and cultural economy, etc.) often and necessarily pulls study into quite disparate contexts of scholarship. My book is not an exercise in corrective integration, which would be both facile and futile, nor does it presuppose a distinct community of enquiry, an established or emergent 'television studies' (see Brunsdon 1997 on variations and tendencies here in recent years). My usage here is plural in spirit not singular and my sense of the study of television internationally suggests the appropriateness of this way of seeing things. However, it is my purpose to make some connections across a span of topics and ideas which seem to have significance and interest and which bear on each other, sometimes in convergence and sometimes in opposition, in ways we can profit from examining further.

'Critical' can be used to indicate three rather different things in the context of a book like this. It points to the long-established tradition of criticism as the practice of arts appraisal. It also indicates the calling attention to shortcomings, weaknesses, and limitations. Finally, it can signal what is regarded as of most importance in the development and direction of enquiry and debate. In my title I would like to activate all three meanings, since they all seem appropriate. Elsewhere, my specific usage will, I hope, be clear. The sequence of chapters is from the framing of institution, through the specific representational issues of image, talk, narration, and flow (unlike the others, a chapter heading which itself marks a formative idea in study) to the phase-based categories of production and reception, the overarching notions of pleasure and knowledge, and, finally, the prospects for television in the future. This provides a useful cumulative read, I believe, but I have also given each chapter a good degree of autonomy, allowing for the fact that selective reading, out of sequence, may well be the preferred form of use for many readers.

Before I develop this introductory account in any further detail, something needs to be said about the extent to which it draws on British experience and the perspectives of British study and argument. The book is essentially about ideas and debate, but in order to demonstrate or assess the usefulness of certain ideas and ground my own appraisals, in many chapters I have taken brief examples from my own national television system, a system which has a distinctive history of relating itself to the public and which is now undergoing radical change. In doing so, I have tried to bear in mind readers not familiar with this system and those who, quite understandably, may want to know only as much about it as aids their engagement with the points of my discussion. Throughout the book, the formative and continuing contribution to television studies of American scholars is fully recognized in extensive citation and so is the way in which specific aspects of the television system and television culture of the United States have become strongly international. Nevertheless, it seemed a good idea not to repress the national basis to my own appraisal, since ersatz internationalism is no less attractive than parochial foreclosure and it might well be argued that the integrity of television studies is currently at greater risk from the former. Moreover, observed at points in its formation and at its present moment of change, British television can provide much to illuminate analysis and argument that occur beyond its national boundaries. I hope to have used it to this effect, partly complementing that extensive literature which, with varying degrees of critical self-consciousness (and sometimes none at all!), makes its claims about television exclusively from a base in the American experience.

The discussion of television within different scholarly disciplines has a fifty-year-old history. As television on both sides of the Atlantic established itself as a popular medium in the 1950s, its significance for public life and popular culture inevitably attracted a growing number of studies, either dealing with one of its aspects as just a part of their investigations or making it their primary focus. Since the 1980s, however, the range of academic treatments has seen an exponential growth: a product both of the extent to which television has now become an integral factor of everyday modernity in both its public and private aspects and of a newer, interdisciplinary spirit in the arts and social sciences which has been attracted precisely by the challenge of television's multi-aspectual character as well as by its social importance.

In what follows, I want to develop some points about television and its study which stand as introductory to the book but which also have the role of locating its contents within a broader intellectual landscape. I have chosen to keep the opening chapter lightly referenced, in line with the idea of a commentary which will be given detail and development in subsequent chapters. At the risk of appearing unduly divisive, I want to look at the development of traditions of 'research' within the social sciences and traditions of 'criticism' within the humanities as two distinct modes of intellectual and scholarly engagement with the medium. This is a little simplistic and runs the risk of undervaluing the efforts of scholars who have tried to think about television more inclusively. It will certainly not find the approval of those who believe that even the very recognition of such borderlines is now unhelpful. But in understanding the configuration of ideas and theories about television, I think this is a broad distinction we need to make, whether or not we then wish to bridge it or transcend it.

Television as Research Object

The overwhelming rationale for most research into television has undoubtedly been anxiety about its influence. This was true of the earliest studies and remains the case today, despite there now being many different kinds of research questions concerning influence. We can usefully distinguish between two broad strands of anxiety, which might be labelled the distortion of politics and the displacement of culture, although many researchers have couched their doubts about the medium in more circumspect language. The chapters of this book variously engage with these anxieties in respect of their own primary topics, but it is worth giving them some preliminary attention here since they have been so significant in shaping the intellectual identity of the research field, producing a paradigm within which some have comfortably worked and which others have vigorously resisted.

Before doing so, I want to draw attention to three interrelated aspects of television which continually figure in debate about it, making this different from debate about press, radio, or cinema, with which, nevertheless, it shares much. These aspects are its electronic, visual, and mass/domestic character. Together, they give the present communicative profile of television a reach, potential instantaneity, scopic range, and penetration of everyday living which transcend other media (including current applications of Information Technology) and lie at the heart of so many arguments about television's power. Television is an industrialized way of managing time and space in the production and circulation of recorded images and sounds. Predominantly these images and sounds are 'broadcast' and are viewed in homes. Television is more than this, but we need to hang on firmly to this truth about it, as the linking of technology, productive and distributive organization, and then social conventions of address and portrayal, in following the various routes which debate has taken.

Anxiety about a distortion of politics has varied, from a specific concern about the supply of political information (as, for instance, during elections) to a more comprehensive sense of television as mediating politics in ways which deeply (and negatively) modify political culture and political process. Often, the threat of de-democratization has been perceived: television replacing primary participation with a secondary or even tertiary engagement, in which the tele-presence of politicians within a political theatre of tele-events reconfigures and redefines political structure and action. This is often television seen as a poor substitute, as eroding an achieved level of democratic practice by the offering of a flawed, partial, strategically managed rendering of reality which nevertheless claims high evidential status and receives good levels of credibility from the popular audience. It is important to note that, historically, the argument cannot be about mediation as such, since all democratic systems have required the involvement of media of some kind, although the contrast between a mediated democracy and a (mysterious and ahistorical) unmediated one is occasionally implied. More often, however, it is a *print*-mediated political culture which is regarded as setting the standards from which television has slipped away. So it is the particular character of television's mediation which is at issue, with the emphasis placed on television's distinctive visual and talk formats and on their institutional and economic framing.

Anxieties about the displacement of culture brought about by television have points in common with political anxieties. For a start, they clearly work within a perspective where the net effect of television is registered as loss rather than gain. However, their attention is dispersed more widely across television's generic output and engages more directly with television as a provider of drama and entertainment. I have found it useful to regard television as having both a centrifugal and a centripetal action in relation to culture-at-large. It is centripetal in so far as it is an unprecedented device for pulling in and processing a very wide range of established and emerging cultural features manifest in other areas (e.g. magazines, sport, music, film, and fashion). It is centrifugal in so far as its own cultural reach and impact extend to the widest boundaries of the culture, including the regional, the national, and, in most cases now, the international. This repeated action of ingestion and projection provides television with an extraordinary cultural dynamics. Its scale of surveillance of what is going on in the culture is matched only by its own cultural penetration. In Britain, this has always had a pluralistic dimension (a variety of different tastes being registered and then being developed) such that easy assumptions about homogenization have always been suspect. They are even more so now, when the range of channels becoming available requires both niche surveillance and niche marketing as well as the continuation of mainstream, aggregatory programming.

In the United States, the much stronger role of commercially led entertainment in the development of television, its consequently reduced status as a matter of public sector management, and the more relaxed and confident positioning of popular culture within versions of the national culture, have combined to give arguments about the cultural impact of the medium a distinctive character. As I shall explore further in later chapters, there has perhaps been less cultural anxiety expressed at the level of policy discussion than is the case in many European countries, but there has been a greater amount and intensity of denunciatory critique by intellectuals in a number of different fields.

Research on the cultural consequences of television has sometimes worked with a strongly normative notion of 'culture' as expressive artefacts, raising questions about the links between aesthetic values and ethical and social values. This has brought it close to the tradition of cultural criticism emerging from the arts disciplines. However, most writing on television and culture has used the term primarily in the descriptive, anthropological sense, to indicate a system of meanings and values which includes artistic expression but which extends much further. It follows that whereas in the former strand of work the most important questions will concern the expressive qualities of television programmes and the impact of these upon tastes, values, and standards, the most important questions from the anthropological perspect-ive will concern the ways in which the terms of everyday life (in, for instance, the experiencing of domesticity, friendship, sexuality, material ambition, and leisure) have been changed by television.

Research on television's impact upon culture has often differed from that on television's political impact in its recognition of the symbolic char-acter of the medium, its links with older, indeed ancient, ideas of ritual and myth and the complexity of its relationship to the real. Too often, research on political consequences has worked with reductive ideas about the trans-fer of information and with a view of influence which ignore the ways in which television programmes generate meaning and produce knowledge and pleasure.

Both the political and cultural strands of enquiry I have sketched out above clearly carry assumptions about television as a powerful agency— the research agenda has frequently set about finding out just *how* powerful television is, it has been an agenda concerned with measurement. At one level, the power of television is easy enough to demonstrate. Institutionally, for instance, it has completely changed the nature of the modern entertain-ment industry, impacting on virtually all areas of leisure, particularly sport and popular music. It has also radically shifted the public nature of politics, requiring kinds of party and governmental organization, styles of advocacy, and responses to criticism which are very different from the modes encour-aged within a newspaper-based, or even radio-based, system of mediation.

There are huge national variations here, of course, but the power of televi-sion in these respects is great and demonstrable. It is sometimes an influence achieved in combination with other, non-televisual, factors but the scale of the televisual contribution can frequently be well documented.

However, for both the political and the cultural strands of research, it has been change at the level of the individual viewer which has most often been the primary object of interest. Looking for television-induced change in individuals is, in some measure, a search which reflects the liberal indi-vidualism of much Western political and cultural thinking. In one kind of scenario familiar from early American research, the developing powers of the mass media, conceived of largely in terms of their potentially negative consequences, are pitched against the mind of the individual citizen. 'Influ-ence' becomes the reductionist object of a search guided by the even more reductionist question, of is there influence *or not*?

Such a perspective fails to understand two very important things about television. First of all, it misses the way in which it is culturally constitutive, directly involved in the circulation of the meanings and values out of which a popular sense of politics and culture is made and which also then provides the interpretative resources for viewing. This turns the relationship between a given influential message and a given vulnerable viewer into something of a research fiction. The second thing which is missed is the fact that *all* of the television which we watch will bring about some modification in our knowledge and experience, however minor and temporary. A lazily watched programme about wildlife in Spain may give us information about types of bird that is minimally retained and never employed as practical know-ledge, a programme later that evening on the last days of a cancer sufferer may generate new knowledge and high emotional impact, perhaps subsequently being used in informing our own actions.

Research on influence has been too interested in *one* particular kind of possible influence, the presumed bad and strong influence of material designed to mislead the mind and excite the emotions. In this view of television power it is *all* high mountains—the varying contours of culture are ignored. In the context of the multiple, indirect ways in which cultural meanings are produced in a modern society (an issue discussed further in Chapter 8) the general question of 'influence or not?' risks banality. Enquiry into television's power needs to rid itself of some of the assumptions behind one of its key terms.

What kinds of power? how exercised? in support of what and against what other factors of social structure and action? These are questions which appear regularly in the chapters which follow.

Television and Criticism

Academic television criticism shares many intellectual features with the lines of research sketched out above. As with those, a differentiation between political and cultural emphases can be made, although perhaps with less sharpness. Criticism is also quite frequently informed by fears of cultural damage, making it 'critical' both in the sense that it works within an intellectual tradition of arts analysis and appraisal and in the sense that it is negative about television in whole or in part. In fact, unlike most 'research', where negative hypotheses are carried into enquiries which can nevertheless generate counter-evidence and counter-indications, 'criticism' has frequently moved to evaluation straight away, sustaining this by the citation of examples which are chosen precisely to *prove* not to *test* the judgement. It thus mixes evidence, argument, and assertion in a way which I think has often become a problem and which I discuss further later.

Critical work on television from within the academy has derived its theories, vocabulary, and sense of function extensively from the body of arts criticism in literature, fine art, and, more recently, film. Many writers of critical work have themselves been trained in arts scholarship and although I earlier warned against assuming too sharp a division in an area which has genuinely encouraged interdisciplinarity, it remains the case that few of the television scholars trained in the social sciences have felt inclined to write criticism (perhaps more arts scholars have attempted modes of research) whatever the level of cross-referencing in publications. I take a defining feature of critical activity to be an engagement with the significatory organization of television programmes themselves, with the use of images and language, generic conventions, narrative patterns, and modes of address, to be found there. This requires a reading or analysis which foregrounds the critic's own interpretative resources as a specialist in the medium and does not work with a notion either of 'data' or of 'method' in the manner conventional in the social sciences (with, for instance, their techniques of quantitatively controlled content analysis). Of course, this does not stop the critic making inferences about the social relationships and configurations of value within which television's texts are placed—there has been a long tradition of such text-and-context scholarship in other areas of criticism (Anglo-American literary studies is a notable example). Television criticism has most often wanted to go beyond the textually descriptive and evaluative and to use its observations here as a route to a broader or deeper cultural diagnosis, either of the past or the present.

A further influence has been the tradition of critical theory coming from mid-twentieth-century European social thought (with an emphasis on the work of the Frankfurt School critics of 'mass culture', notably Theodor Adorno (see the reprinted translations in Adorno 1991) and Walter Benjamin (a representative collection is Benjamin 1973). This has provided one route for Marxist ideas to inform television criticism. Another route has been through more recent theories of ideology, of the relations between meaning, social consciousness, and political power, particularly as developed by the French Marxist philosopher Louis Althusser from the 1960s and debated across many disciplines (see Althusser 1971). There has also been a widespread use in criticism of the theory of 'hegemony', a theory about the way in which the terms of popular political consent are, in fact, managed by dominant class groupings in their own interests. Ideas about hegemonic processes, particularly about the importance of cultural factors to their success, were developed by the Italian political theorist and activist, Antonio Gramsci in the 1920s but only translated into English in the early 1970s (Gramsci 1971). Feminist theories of the social order and of subjectivity and consciousness, variously aligned or opposed to Marxist ideas, also provided important new conceptual resources and a revision of *purpose* to much critical work. They questioned established protocols of analysis and encouraged a stronger self-awareness in critical studies (see the account in Brunsdon 1993, the overview in Mumford 1997, and the collected essays in Brunsdon *et al.* 1997).

Since the 1980s, much work in arts criticism has moved away from even the most modified forms of Marxist critique towards the broad and varied terms of postmodernist thinking. It has either judged the condition of postmodernity to pose questions about discourse, self, and social order to be of a different kind from the ones posed by the modernist societies within which critical Marxism developed or it has found the intellectual ferment of postmodernist ideas to have superseded, beyond revision, modes of Marxist thinking. It is worth registering the difference between these two ways of becoming post-Marxist and postmodern in orientation, even if in practice they appear mutually entailed. Not surprisingly, television, with those features of space–time manipulation, social displacement, and scopic appeal discussed above, has often been regarded as an agency of postmodern culture, despite its origins as a modernist cultural technology. It has been seen as the representational hub of a new pattern of knowledge and feeling and of new kinds of political organization, self-consciousness, and identity. Such claims are discussed at many points throughout this book.

I want to conclude these preliminary points on television criticism by noting very briefly the broad critical approaches taken by three writers on the medium who have had a considerable impact on critical ideas about it—Marshall McLuhan, Raymond Williams, and John Fiske. All three writers are mentioned in subsequent chapters as particular issues in their work come under discussion.

Marshall McLuhan located television within a cultural criticism giving emphasis to the 'techno-sensory' character of new media, to their function as 'extensions' of primary experience. Relatively unconcerned either with content, programme form, or with substantive social context, McLuhan focuses on the deep consequences of exposure to the *medium*. Arguing for television as a medium encouraging high viewer participation, McLuhan (for example, 1964) presents television both as exciting and as ambiguous in cultural value. In general, and well against the tendency of later critics, McLuhan resolves the ambiguity in the direction of television's positive potential. Here he is talking of television and the child:

> The TV image, that is to say, even more than the icon, is an extension of the sense of touch. Where it encounters a literate culture, it necessarily thickens the sense-mix, transforming fragmented and specialist extensions into a seamless web of experience. (McLuhan 1973: 358)

A comparison which for many critics leads to judgement on the failure of television to honour the standards of literate culture becomes, for McLuhan, a celebration of the new richnesses of holistic experience which television brings and which the institutions of the literate culture will tend to constrain. This championing of television, however qualified, undoubtedly enhanced McLuhan's guru status within the television industry at the same time as his sense of the 'new as good' made his writings attractive to a young television generation. His benign visionary approach has been hard to follow, even by the most optimistic writers, although his generalized attention to the links between technology and culture has led to his rediscovery by some scholars attempting to respond to the radical changes brought about by information technology systems.

Raymond Williams, like McLuhan, worked from a base in literary criticism. Indeed, both of them had been influenced by the Cambridge teacher F. R. Leavis, who had from the 1930s pursued his own distinctive account of the art–society relationship. Like McLuhan, Williams too is interested in Technology. What makes *Television: Technology and Cultural Form* (1974) so distinctive is the way he takes 'technology' as the category with which to *open* a study of television and as something which needs a new kind of critical enquiry in its relations to cultural change. However, unlike McLuhan's, Williams's account of television as a technology is thoroughly historical and social. The exploration of the tensions between the socially conservative and the socially innovative aspects of television is perhaps one of the most original strands in Williams's account. Another theme not found in McLuhan is his emphasis on the relationship to commerce and to commercial imperatives as these affect the organization of schedules, the selection of content, and the development of forms. Williams discusses the medium as positioned within both state and commercial spheres, its history is the product of sometimes conflicting policies and strategies, often having unforeseen consequences. His tone of cautious optimism about what television can bring to the nature of public life, particularly to the further achievement of democratic society, is worked for in a sometimes dense internal argument with those negative factors which, drawing on both British and American experience, he also wishes to document. This is in contrast to the relative ease and expansive phrasing with which McLuhan reaches his general, upbeat judgements.

John Fiske's *Television Culture* (1987) offers a synoptic account which partly consolidated and then helped further to establish a particular version of television studies in Britain and the United States. Unlike Williams, whose discussion is cast largely in terms of the issue of public knowledge, Fiske approaches television within a framing of ideas about popular culture and about pleasure. This entails a recasting of issues of public knowledge within a broader sense of television's forms and uses. Fiske follows Williams and others in assessing television as a kind of commodity production but, compared with many other writers, he greatly increases the attention given to television as a semiotic practice, a particular usage of signs. The wide range of ideas about popular culture and sign-systems which is drawn on in Fiske's account make his commentary less grounded than that of Williams. 'Television' as text and 'television culture' as kinds of viewing experience develop a certain autonomy from particular institutions and specific social settings. In adopting what he sees as a 'viewer-centred' approach, emphasizing the ways in which audiences seek to make what they watch fit their own experiences and lives, Fiske is inclined to celebrate rather than criticize the interplay of programming with everyday life. In this, he is closer to McLuhan than to Williams, who returns regularly to the need for major reform.

All three of these writers offer an account of television as a system of public symbolism, the extent and density of its depictions merging technology, craft, and art in utterly new ways, permeating the culture with its images, sounds, and story patterns. The critical perspective, with its openness to television as meaning-making, is a necessary one to maintain and develop. The sustained scrutiny of criticism and its concern with aesthetics, discourse, and value will continue to expand our sense of what television is and is becoming. The strands of social research address the medium in its more objectifiable aspects, seeking to increase the range and quality of our knowledge about its organization and functioning. To declare the two projects to be complementary may be to fudge the issue of their intellectual differences and their sometimes awkward overlaps. Throughout this book and in its very design I have, however, worked with the idea that a stronger sense of mutual interest, dialogue, and accountability would be valuable.

I will finish this introductory chapter by saying something about the status of theory in television studies. The theoretical is a necessary dimension both of research and of criticism and therefore my previous discussion has been very much concerned with it. In the chapters which follow, theoretical matters are often a primary consideration. Yet questions of theory have sometimes become detached from specific enquiry to the point where theory has been seen as a virtually autonomous realm of academic interest in television, the theorist being distinguishable from researchers and critics as a result of the high generality of their engagement and their exclusive emphasis on ideas rather than the interplay between ideas and kinds of evidence or analysis. There is certainly a place for 'general theory' in the study of television; for one thing it allows for a wider and more imaginative interconnection with the thinking which is developing in other fields of study than does conceptual work rooted in specific enquiry. There is no doubt that the ferment of ideas which the arts and social sciences have seen over the last two decades has made a primarily theoretical interest in television seem both exciting and intellectually productive.

Yet problems have followed from the attractiveness and growth of a television theory regarded as a separate and sometimes premier sphere rather than a dimension of all good study. An over-privileged idea of theory has introduced too much self-serving assertion, elaboration, and obscurity into debate (a problem explored further in Corner 1997). What might be admitted either as countervailing evidence or argument to the positions advanced by theory has often been hard or even impossible to assess. As a result, the field has shown a tendency to proliferate theories rather than provide for a vigorous exchange of ideas. The end of this introduction is not a good place for condensed polemics and in several of the chapters which follow I attempt to assess issues of theorization in relation to particular areas of study. However, in choosing the term 'ideas' for the title of this book I hope to give support to the more genuinely argumentative ways of thinking and writing about television.

2

Institution

THE word 'institution' primarily indicates a widely acknowledged aspect of television rather than a critical idea about it. Nevertheless, despite this straightforward descriptive meaning, 'institution' has also often carried an analytic and sometimes a polemical inflection in the academic literature. There are three related reasons for this. First of all, an emphasis on television's institutionality has often been set against other research concerns, sometimes with the implication of applying a corrective or at least a balance to the directions in which these other concerns lead. Secondly, the way in which institutional factors should relate, causally and consequentially, to other aspects of television has caused considerable debate. Thirdly, the very question of what should be taken into account in considering television as an institution, and *how* it should be taken into account, has been found a challenge even amongst those who have wished to give the institutional dimension priority in their studies. In this chapter, then, I want to explore what is involved in the consideration of television as institution.

To regard television institutionally is to regard it within the forms of its historical and social establishment and organization. Television, unlike poetry, say, cannot exist *non*-institutionally since even its minimal resource, production, and distribution requirements are such as to require high levels of organization in terms of funding, labour, and manufacturing process. As I shall suggest later, there are contrary shifts both towards aggregation and dispersal in the current pattern of international television. Among other things, these may have the effect of altering the relationship between what we now think of as the public processes of 'television' and what we think of as the more privatized processes of 'video' (e.g. home, surveillance, and corporate). However, television has become installed in most modern societies in terms of an institutional ecology—major national corporations, networks, international corporate giants, small independents, local stations—which will retain its basic features for some time to come.

A more abstract and analytic way of seeing television institutionally, rather than simply pointing to the fact of corporations, companies, production houses, etc., is to focus on the way in which institutional forms act as a matrix for, and a nexus between, the various constituents of television. Institutions give the processes of television (including viewing experience) their specificity, a specificity with a historical, national character which is the product of given political, social, and cultural factors interacting with available technology. Whilst it is by no means possible to trace all the processes of television by holding an institutional focus, there is a sense in which such a focus serves to condense many features of process—identified elsewhere in terms of programme form or of viewing behaviour—back into structure and practice. By way of illustration, we can take three very different examples, operating at distinct levels, of the nexus function—that between funding, product, and use; that between public and private; and that between knowledge and pleasure.

Institutions act to interconnect funding, product, and use because of the strategic play-off between their investment in specific projects at the levels of station, channel, and programme and their need to gauge audience responses correctly enough to make these projects, and products, viable at a given level of production cost. The insertion (often massive) of advertising income into funding can only be maintained if viewing levels and viewing profiles support it. In a sense, many television institutions, whether funded by advertising or not, act as a junction point between the vectors of supply led demand (what it is in the best interests and profits of the institution to produce, then strongly marketed to viewers) and those of demand-led supply (what specific groups of viewers like and what they don't like, what they will and will not watch, fed back as the recipes for successful production, further development, and profitability). They are therefore best seen as the sites of political and cultural interplay and of 'brokerage' rather than as agencies primarily either of imposition or of a consumerist response to demand.

The changing definition of, and linkage between, the public and the private has been seen by many commentators (for instance, Scannell 1989; Fornas 1995; Thompson 1995) to be one of the most significant consequences of broadcasting, particularly of television, and a key characteristic of late modernity. The way in which the realm of public affairs has taken on domestic, familial registers (as for instance in contemporary performances of political celebrity and in the modes of address of television reportage, increasingly influenced by the contexts of home viewing) and in which what was previously considered private has become open for public debate (as for instance in a whole range of issues concerning sexuality, where soap operas and the newer forms of chat show have often been pioneers) has not simply reconfigured the relationship between these two categories but put into question the usefulness of continuing to recognize the division they indicate. It is the institutionality of television—its interplays of social class tastes, of traditional with emergent cultural forms, of official with popular perspectives, of varieties of talk—which must receive our attention if we wish to see how such broad shifts and displacements have been initiated, reflected, adapted, and amplified.

The generic system of television is also an important classifier of the 'light' and the 'serious' in modern culture, of what can be (and what cannot) be considered comic. The steady increase in the various televisual manifestations of irony, of the obliquely funny, of the double-take, and the frame within a frame, is testimony to television's engagement with post-traditional uncertainties in this area, as is its extensive involvement in the emergence of a 'camp' sensibility within the range of popular pleasures (Ross 1989 discusses the various elements at work here). Such classifications are subject to regular, and sometimes quite radical, revision. Related to them is the differentiation between knowledge and entertainment, a division which, always blurry, has now virtually collapsed within the newer formats of international television, generating hybrids which, not surprisingly, often project most strongly their entertaining possibilities (see Kilborn 1994; Dahlgren 1995; and Corner 1995).

Right from the earliest days of television, there was debate about its essential character as a medium and therefore about how best to institutionalize it as an industry and a national service. In his study of the early American developments, William Boddy (1990: 23) notes how the possibility of 'theatre television', playing to assembled audiences on large screens, was considered a serious alternative to domestic possibilities in the 1940s. There was also extensive debate about the extent to which television would draw on the distinctive traditions of radio broadcasting and of cinema in achieving its best, and most profitable, mix. Clearly, there were clear national variations, too, in thinking about television's function. The American model followed the precedent of earlier broadcasting in regarding the medium as providing a radical extension of the entertainment industry, with private finance and advertising revenue as the chief source of funding. The British model followed its own radio precedent in placing emphasis on the responsibilities (and exciting new potential) for public information and education, within a system where a licence fee indirectly funded a public corporation. John Caughie (1991b: 22) quotes a pioneer British producer, Gerald Cock, noting in 1936 that:

> television is, from its very nature, more suitable for the dissemination of all kinds of information than for entertainment as such, since it can scarcely be expected to compete successfully with films in that respect.

Elements of either model can be found in the other and both incorporated a range of informational, fictional, and variously diverting formats, but this early difference in the form of institutionalization has had a significant influence on the subsequent history of television's development, and on its political, social, and cultural profile, elsewhere in the world. I shall draw selectively on the experience of the American model throughout this chapter, but the idea of institution embeds debate in the history and nature of specific broadcasting systems perhaps more quickly than any of my other chapter headings and I want to give some space, too, to the British and European models and their problems.

When a comparison is made between television as an institution and the three other major media—press, radio, and cinema—a number of differentiating factors become obvious, some of which I have touched on above. The institutional status and function of the press has, in most countries, been significantly displaced or at least radically modified by broadcasting services as the latter have become the principal sources of public information and the chief arena for political expression and for political theatre. The institutional profile of the press is often grounded in a plurality of complementary and/or competing products. This is the basis of classic liberal theory about how the press can work best—as the realization of a 'free market-place of ideas'. The phrase is derived from the thinking of eighteenth-century philosophers of liberalism, particularly John Stuart Mill, where the idea of the market is essentially a metaphor, although the link between free market structures and freedom of expression is central both to past and present debate.

In practice, the problems here have often concerned the transformation of inequalities of wealth into inequalities of informational and publicity power, with a subsequent need for public controls to correct market-produced imbalances seen to be injurious to the democratic process. The apparent paradox of regulating for freedom, with its consequent institutional tensions between public bodies and private companies has become the focus for controversy and debate in many national newspaper systems.

In European broadcasting, however, the centralizing of national informational resources within a very small number of organizations, many having direct links with the state, has often raised very different problems concerning the public interest. Here, the market, rather than being the mechanism which needs correcting by other means, has often been regarded itself as the means of correction. As the tendency towards deregulation and privatization in telecommunications continues internationally (see Mosco 1996) the contexts for television's institutionality may come more closely to resemble the competitive (and potentially distortive) pluralism of the press, in relation to which a measure of 'public' controls has sometimes to be reasserted in the interests of a sense of communicative equity, of a greater equality of access and representation across the political and cultural community. However, the proportionally much higher costs of entry into this market will continue to work against the level of proliferation and variety which the press, at least in some countries, is able to display. Where entry costs are a reduced obstacle, as in certain cable and community television systems, the problem often remains of achieving a level of production quality which can be competitive with established, and expected, industry standards, based on strong resourcing in equipment, staffing, and production budgets.

Radio is often positioned at a middle point in the spectrum here. In Britain, for instance, radio has retained a good measure of its older institutional identity as a national broadcasting medium with an inclusive, broad audience, whilst at the same time it has established itself over the last thirty years as a key component of local public communications and is now in the process of partial reinstitutionalization as a much more various (and print-like) channel for the delivery of commercially funded, narrowcast programming to identified audience sectors at local, regional, and national levels. All these shifts have brought changes in programme concepts and the speech relationships with audiences by which radio broadcasting gains its identity. These changes are being paralleled in television as diversification and dispersal take place there too.

As many writers have noted, the contrast with cinema is a sharper one. For a start, cinema was developed with an informational role marginal to the main business of fictional entertainment. Thus, the public obligations which are laid upon press, radio, and television as a result of their journalistic functions have rarely featured directly in discussion of cinema's operations, despite the widespread existence of political and ethical censorship. Moreover, as a result of the institutional division between production and exhibition and the focus on the consumptional unit of the film rather the channel/schedule, the site of cinema's institutionality is as much the cinema itself, the *place* for visits, as the studio system. It is perhaps the most significant feature of television, widely noted and researched, that it engages the viewer in the spaces and times of the home, thereby following radio in developing not only a strong domestic aesthetic for programmes (see the discussion of this in Chapter 8) but also an institutional persona in which home-friendly attributes are an essential feature, however combined with other qualities.

I want to look more closely at the institutional character of television by considering it in four important aspects—technology, economy, politics, and culture. That these overlap, quite apart from the definitional questions they might beg, I readily agree. But they provide a useful way of exploring issues currently posed for television research and for contemplating the forms which television may take in the future.

Institutional Character of Television

■ Technology

Recent developments in the production, distribution, and reception of television systems have begun to change the social and cultural profile of television so much, albeit with great national variations, that research often seems to be focusing on a moving target. As a consequence, awareness of technology, the registering of technology as a key factor in television's institutional identity, is much stronger than it has been in the past. The spread of satellite and cable and the rapid increase in the use of domestic video recorders have for many audiences changed the televisual experience in ways which nearly all studies have had to take account of. Together with the newer density of technology–culture relations prompted by advancements in information technology, particularly by the arrival of the internet, such developments have led to a new, intensive research focus. It is no longer possible for studies simply to regard the technology of television as a given, whose institutional implications are self-evident and whose applications do not require independent investigation.

Among British scholars, Raymond Williams stands out not only for the emphasis which he places on the institutional forms of television right from the start of his writings on the medium (an unusual emphasis for a literary critic continuing to pursue primarily textual studies), but also for his focus on technology. In his classic mid-1970s study *Television: Technology and Cultural Form* (1974), the subtitle signals the decisive focus, briefly discussed in my introductory chapter. In fact, of the six chapters in the book, four of them have the word 'technology' in their titles and the account of 'cultural form' proceeds by way of two chapters which attempt to establish broader interrelations between television as institution, technology, and society. It is significant that this book was largely written whilst Williams was a visiting professor in California, encountering forms of television and emerging technologies (his host university, Stanford, had a special interest here) which would certainly not have pressed themselves on his awareness in Britain. This gives the book something of a prophetic character for the British situation not only in respect of substantive developments but also in terms of theoretical engagement. In Chapter 6 I look in detail at the influential ideas about 'flow' which are put forward in a central section. However, the principal question which Williams poses in the early part of the book is about the interplay of shaping influences between technological potential and particular applications and adoptions informed by political and commercial advantage. Williams is particularly keen to expose two, complementary, fallacies. First of all, the fallacy of a technological determinism which assumes a direct effect ('impact') of technology upon society, regarding the properties of a technology as somehow intrinsic and non-social. Secondly, the fallacy of a 'symptomatic technology', which assumes that technological development is largely the by-product of social forces, a realm subordinate to other features of society and with a quasi-accidental character. Of these, it is clearly the former which is still the more pervasive and the more various in its terms of expression, having gained something of a new lease of life as an active ideology following a decade of techno-cultural change of unprecedented scale and complexity.

In a way which prefigures much current writing, both in its themes and its difficulties, Williams wants to avoid what he sees as the basic mistake of 'isolating' technology yet nevertheless to hold on to its specificity within the whole process of social change. He ends his relevant section thus:

> Such an interpretation would differ from technological determinism in that it would restore *intention* to the process of research and development . . . At the same time the interpretation would differ from symptomatic technology in that these purposes and practices would be seen as *direct*; as known social needs, purposes and practices to which the technology is not marginal but central. (Williams 1974: 14)

However, actually plotting the causality of development in any given case, particularly the degrees and kinds of 'direct intention', remains a good deal harder than this might suggest. For instance, the emergence of cable rather than satellite as the principal means of extension of range and choice to British viewers in the 1990s is the combination of a number of government and corporate intentions, some a good deal less direct than others (on this, see Collins and Murroni 1996), in combination with factors of happenstance. As the television industry becomes subject to further internal differentiation, including that of institutional functions which were once unified, specific causal routes may become even less clear to analysis. An added factor here will be the degree of convergence with other parts of the telecommunications industry, most importantly the electronic data networks and their various corporate and domestic applications. In Chapter 11 I review the present and imminent situation more thoroughly.

Whilst there have been many momentous shifts in television's production technology, undoubtedly the single most important change in consumption practices to date has followed the domestic availability of the video cassette recorder. Now extensive in use, the VCR has not only permitted the 'time-shifting' which frees the viewer from transmission schedules and also allows simultaneous transmissions to be taken into the home, but it has also opened up the screen to pre-recorded entertainments, thereby stimulating another sector of the film/video market. Williams used the suggestive phrase 'mobile privatization' (1974: 26) when describing the way in which the institution of television had reinforced tendencies of social change being produced else where in the culture. These tendencies were towards a kind of domesticized individualism set within a complex of abstract, public systems. The changes brought about by the VCR, when combined with the new availability of multi-channel systems and the imminent emergence of an array of IT applications, will have the effect of radically increasing the privatization of television, a point now being recognized in the priorities of international television research.

■ **Economy** How television is paid for and the subsequent implications this has for programming policy and for the programmes themselves have rightly been considered matters of the utmost importance. It was noted earlier that the split between a 'public' model drawing on a licence fee and a 'commercial' model drawing on advertising and sponsorship has characterized the different, early trajectory of television institutions in Britain and the United States. In Britain, there was a tradition of strong and proactive public service controls being exercised over the operations of commercial stations and channels.

The rather hybridic model of grafting public service responsibilities and oversight controls on to a system run in the primary interests of commercial profit looks unlikely to survive for long, either in Britain (where it is in obvious decline) or in other areas of the world where there has been an attempt to follow the example. Deregulation and privatization (see Garnham 1990; Mosco 1996; Burgelman 1997) have been dominant tendencies of the 1990s, removing perceived impediments to market development. Although governments have often presided over deregulation in the interests of improved product quality and range, few analysts in the industry or in the academic sector have failed to note the underlying economic rationale. Even in the United States, a new phase of strategic restructuring within the telecommunications sector has been perceived to put the political and cultural adequacy of television under new pressure (see the accounts in Mosco 1996 and Herman and McChesney 1997).

However, the extent to which the output of a television system can be predicted from its funding base remains an issue of debate within television research. The question of the level of public regulation which is then actually required to offset certain tendencies and encourage others gives it strong policy implications. Much commentary (for example, Keane 1991) has worked with the idea of 'commodification' as the fundamental problem to which only 'decommodified' levels of institutional policy and practice provide an answer. However, quite apart from the strong degree of impracticality entailed in pitching the argument in these terms, there is as yet insufficient address to the degrees and kinds of commodification which television systems and their output display and the extent to which commodity values can coexist with other values in the same channel or programme. Within the British experience, admittedly that of a regulated market, commercial television was soon responding to the wider range of national cultural factors, and registering new kinds of cultural energy, much more freely than the BBC. One could argue that this was as much a matter of its commercial logic as of any philosophy of inclusion, but its effect was to change the BBC's own programming policy and to contribute significantly to the development of television as a popular medium (see the accounts in Corner 1991). Moreover, the condemnation of commercial systems through their guilt by association with advertising is no longer such a self-evident argument as it once appeared to many academics. For it is not at all clear that advertising constitutes a pernicious 'magic system' (Williams 1960) which is routinely effective in seducing people into false needs and false values. Allowing high levels of television funding to be drawn from advertising (national or international) may, however, work against the optimum use of television as an agency of the public sphere (see below). Arguments about achieving effective levels of public accountability over commercially funded systems are likely to provide the most important focus of dialogue between policy-makers and researchers in the next few years. Emerging forms of the relationship between funding, regulation, and programming in Central and Eastern Europe will be a significant feature of the international debate (an issue usefully explored in Downing 1996 and Sparks 1998).

■ **Politics**   However institutionalized, television is inescapably a political agency. As a system of public communication, it quickly comes to complement, and then partially to displace, the functions of press and radio. Regardless of their mode of funding and regulation, or their degree of commitment to entertainment, most television systems have a political core as a result of the journalism they sustain—their routine provision of 'the news'. Even in societies where a state-controlled system ensures conformity with government views, the claim is still that the news acts as the resource for the constitution of an informed public, a popular engagement with national developments and the expression of popular political opinions, however managed and uniform these turn out to be.

In the contrasting case of societies with a high level of open political dissent, few national television systems have allowed the journalism they carry to project explicit party political affiliations (although there have been some interesting attempts to institutionalize sectional interest and pressure group commentary through regular slots and even channel ownership). This situation has resulted in a wide range of different kinds of legislation regarding the 'balance', 'objectivity', and 'impartiality' of broadcast journalism and recurrent debates about the implementation of such principles in journalistic practice (see the synoptic account in Corner 1995).

As the institutional character of television moves closer to that of the press—a range of competing channels of provision sharing the market at national, regional, and local levels—the political obligations placed upon its journalism may be modified. However, the practices of news journalism themselves have, internationally, been institutionalized as part of the democratic process and they thus have a degree of independence from shifts in the institutionalizing of television. It will be interesting to see what latitude in declared role and in performance is actually exercised by journalism as a result of these shifts (see Dahlgren 1995 and MacManus 1994 for a review of different tendencies here, and also Chapter 10 of this volume).

■ **Culture**   Television's identity as a cultural agency is more dispersed than its political identity, which often derives substantially from its journalism although it, too, needs to be considered across a broader generic range. I remarked in my introductory chapter how 'culture' can be used in two different, if related, ways when applied to television. First of all it can be used as a broad synonym for the arts, including the popular arts, and entertainment. Here the relationship with national arts policy is highlighted as well as the relationship with the arts and entertainment industries and their specific publics. Of course, much that appears on television is 'cultural' in this sense and television has become a major cultural producer as well as giving access to extra-televisual cultural performances. In Britain, as I have suggested, it has been instrumental in developing versions of the national and the popular and in realigning relationships between the 'high' and the 'low' and between the subsidized and the commercial. But, following work in anthropology and cultural studies, the term can also be used more broadly to indicate the organization of values and meanings to be found in a society, where an extensive array of questions about the medium and its influence on social identity, attitudes, values, and tastes are then raised. In some current usages of a term like 'popular culture' it is often hard to tell which meaning is privileged and despite their undoubted interconnection the result is sometimes confusion. Here, I shall refer to both dimensions of culture, but I shall give most attention to the first, more limited, meaning since discussion of the broader, more diffuse, meaning is to be found at many points throughout the book.

National histories of broadcasting vary considerably in the degree to which radio and then television were perceived by institutional controllers to be instruments of national culture. The British model, initially articulated by Lord Reith in respect of BBC radio services in the 1920s, was self-consciously one of cultural improvement. The institutional requirement, as perceived by Reith, was for a national monopoly to be enjoyed by the BBC in order to ensure universal availability but also to allow that 'one general policy may be maintained throughout the country and definite standards promulgated' (see the full citation in Scannell and Cardiff 1991: 8). In pursuit of this emphatically productionist perspective on services (the notion of audience demand is a secondary consideration at best), Reith opposed the introduction of commercial television in the 1950s. However, his case was a more awkward one to argue in the changed cultural climate of postwar Britain than it had been in the 1920s. It was seen quite widely as a dictatorial position, essentially undemocratic and unwilling, as one prominent advocate of competition put it, to allow people to decide for themselves 'whether they want to be educated or entertained in the evening' (Lloyd 1951). Yet despite the arrival of commercial competition, British television policy still frequently pursued policies of cultural education and the implicit endorsement of cultural standards of a kind not so evident in systems where the degree of dependence on advertising revenue led to schedules and programmes which brought a relatively quick return on investment.

The industrial interconnections which now exist internationally between television and, for example, the popular music industry, the film industry, and a wide variety of national sports mean that, quite independently of any cultural policies to which its institutions may commit themselves, it operates as a major institutional nexus for arts and leisure.

The emerging new order of television culture is likely to be more international than the programme diets it replaces, but it is also likely to bring with it a higher degree of cultural segmentation (including that by class and income) and perhaps less opportunities for taste-shifting and taste-mixing than earlier public models of broadcasting attempted to provide. These are matters given further scrutiny in later chapters.

Television as Institution and the Public Sphere

The notion of 'the public sphere', derived from the writings of the German philosopher Jurgen Habermas (see, for instance, Habermas 1989) has undoubtedly been the most influential idea in recent media research on policy and institutions and it may help us to keep the issues of technology, economics, politics, and culture interconnected. Its definition and application, particularly to the historical development of media systems, have received a vast amount of exposition and debate (for television, Dahlgren 1995 offers a useful overview whilst Peters 1993 provides a good critical evaluation). The notion of the 'public sphere' points to the requirement for democratic societies to sustain a space for the circulation of information, the exchange of opinion, and the conducting of debate. This space should exist independently of the institutions of the state and it should also be free, too, from the constraints of private, corporate interests. It is, in a sense, a space which provides for, and encourages, the practice of rational citizenship. Although illustrative use is made of earlier periods in political history (particularly the bourgeois literary-intellectual culture of eighteenth-century London) Habermas presents a normative ideal rather than a tight prescription for practice. However, it is an ideal which has been found attractive and useful by writers on media policy. Many of those who have used it have had, nevertheless, to recognize both its inclination towards an overly rationalistic account of political and social action, underplaying affective factors (see Scannell 1989) and, more importantly, a relative lack of engagement with issues of gender (Fraser 1990 offers a detailed reappraisal; see also the discussion in Mclaughlin 1993).

Habermas is particularly keen to draw attention to the direct relationship between the rise of 'publics' and the development of the means of 'publicity'. Once societies develop in their modern form, 'publics' are dependent upon—in part they are the constructions of—the means of publicity, for only through such means can knowledge and opinion become 'public' and citizens recognize themselves as member of such a grouping. Habermas is deeply pessimistic about the way in which modern communications systems —in sharp contrast to what he sees as the radical, reasoning, participatory tradition of the early newspaper—have become instruments of misinformation and of élite power, substantive debate being largely displaced by spectacle and participation by spectatorship.

At several points throughout this book I shall have occasion to refer to Habermas's ideas as they have variously informed writing and research on television, particularly on the kinds of discourse which it carries and the modes of popular knowledge which it sustains. However, here I would simply want to point to the obvious institutional implications which the broad idea of the public sphere holds for television. Television, by the very nature of its depictive flows, is involved in the constitution and maintenance of the contemporary public. Its publicness and its politicality cannot be comprehensively reconfigured as private, even though its funding, its profusion of channels, and, indeed, some aspects of its content combine to give it a stronger private profile than was provided by the national corporations and networks of an earlier stage of its development. The choice for national and international policy is essentially either to recognize, and engage with, its characteristics and functions as a medium of public culture and polity or to ignore and perhaps even to disguise these even as they continue, unacknowledged, to shape the terms of the national and international political order and the frameworks of cultural value.

In grappling with the levels of institutional issue raised by Habermas, however, the very meaning which can be placed on 'public' in the 1990s has proved contentious. Much of the British writing on the institutions of television has drawn on the notion of public with relative confidence. For example, in the work of Raymond Williams, it is the radical extension and deepening of existing public service principles which is called for. American critiques have often worked with an implicit sense of an absent but needed public service model. This is sometimes complicated by a strong, national perception of the productive mutuality of individual freedoms and vigorous commercial activity and also by a suspicion of overarching normative bodies.

In the British commentary of the 1970s and 1980s, the need for a more thorough revision of the idea as well as the practice of public service television starts to be noted, with questions of class and gender discrimination (increasingly, those of ethnicity too) being raised against the dominant corporate formulations of public value as well as against the record of practice (see Garnham 1990). More recently, the whole question of thinking through an adequate notion of public broadcasting has not only been troubled by the rapid and extensive shift to privatization. It has become caught up in larger questions about the forms of the public which it is now desirable or even possible for any public institution to represent. John Keane (1995) expresses this more pluralist sense of public life, in which a mosaic of different communities and interest groupings of varying size, working at different levels of formality and within a mix of institutional frameworks, replaces the focus on a single, unified public which has certainly been the unproblematic starting-point of much policy formulation and critique. Keane's distrust of the generalized imperatives of the Public Good and of the conventional forms of assertion and defence of public values coincides at points with the feminist critique of Fraser (1990).

In response to Keane's arguments, Nicholas Garnham (1995) has made the important point that, whatever the increasing complexity and pluralism of public sites in society, 'the territorially-based state' remains 'the major site and source of political power' (Garnham 1995: 24). He notes 'It is only here that claims can be translated into legitimated political claims on the whole polity, backed ultimately by the redistributive and coercive powers of the state.'

It is likely that television will become much further implicated in the pluralization of public life and the changing terms of citizenship responsibilities and rights (on these, see for instance Gray 1995). Its further extension as an agency of individualized leisure will be a factor in this shift. The impact will be felt more strongly in those countries which, like Britain, have a history of attempts at harnessing the regulation and conduct of broadcasting to ideas of national identity and unity (or, more recently, a nervous unity-in-difference). But television, even in its newly dispersed forms, also remains connected in numerous ways to the 'site and source of political power' too, to the processes of legitimation and political claims-making. As I noted above, its public character, though it will change, will not disappear simply because it is no longer officially recognized. The particular combination of plurality and unity active in its changing public status across politics and culture will provide the focus both for academic debate and policy deliberation.

In Europe, it is difficult to see the institutions of public service surviving without a high level of accommodating flexibility (Chapter 11 reviews the present situation further). The United States, with its greater tolerance of aggressive commercial diversity and lower levels of public oversight in the telecommunications sector, will address changes within a stronger sense of continuity and with different assumptions about the limits of the possible and the desirable. Nevertheless, a steady reconfiguration both of the institutional nature of television and the terms for assessing its performance is likely to occur here too.

In this chapter, I have attempted to address those aspects of television-as-institution which seem to me most important for the development of ideas and analysis. Elsewhere in this book, the issues are developed further in the specific connections of institution to practice and process, but everywhere in it they are relevant.

3
Image

VARIETIES of image constitute the hub of television as a medium (literally, 'seeing at a distance'). It is properties of the image which fascinate and attract, which become the focus for debate about sexually explicit and violent content, which are featured in most discussion of advertising and of the displacement of political substance by 'presentation'. The images which television can offer, and particularly the development of possibilities in content and in form of depiction, are central elements in determining the commodity value which programmes have in the television market-place. Those who have written about the ideological function of television (for example, Feuer 1983; Fiske 1987) have regarded the combination of pleasure and illusion of television's images to be the key to its efficiency in this respect, both in factual and fictional programming. Such critiques have connected with more general commentary about the dominance of professionally produced images in the public culture of late modern society, a dominance often seen as negative in its overall consequences, establishing a 'regime' of appearances and impoverishing the resources of critical imagination.

The television image is an instance, one might say now the classic instance, of the electronic image. It is also usually the moving image and, as a consequence, the edited image. All three of these dimensions give to television's picturing activity a distinctive semiotic profile, distinguishing it from the photographic and cinematic texts with which it nevertheless keeps close, if generically varied, relations. Further exploration of each dimension is a useful way into the central issues of this chapter.

The Electronic Image

Television's image is produced by a recording process, different from, but comparable with, that of photography. Objects in front of the television camera are registered by the light rays entering the camera lens. This registration is scanned and turned into electronic information for sequential and rapid ('instantaneous') transmission and recording or reception by a television set, at which point the information is converted back line by line into a picture again. Such a process gives to the television image a certain ontological character, its own being is in a direct causal relationship to the being of that which it represents (e.g. the presenter's head, the busy market square, the football field, the occupants of the car). Even allowing for the development of digital image manipulation, producing the image more as construct than as record, the evidential implications of this process are still strong and affect the communicative profile of television deeply and in a number of ways, especially as a medium of non-fiction. Photography and cinema also possess comparable properties of image production and around them there has gathered a rich and complex literature of commentary on ontological and evidential matters (see, for example, Bazin 1967; Barthes 1977; Carroll 1996). However, unlike photography or cinema, there is also the possibility of 'instant' transmission in television, providing the medium with that 'liveness' which has been seen to be its defining characteristic, even if with the advent of production recording it was no longer the routine necessity which it had been in the early years. The 'liveness' of television is related to the strong sense of distant seeing which the medium generates, together with the fascinations of seeming close. A medium unable to produce anything but recorded images does not produce the temporal alignment (happening-as-you-watch) upon which the special magic of distant seeing is premissed and around which the energies of many Outside Broadcast pioneers were focused.

Writing in 1936, the British pioneer television producer, Gerald Cock, estimated the appeal of live television against film in uncompromising terms:

> I believe viewers would rather see an actual scene of rush hour at Oxford Circus directly transmitted to them than the latest in film musicals costing £100,000. (cited in Caughie 1991*b*: 23)

It is hard to surpass this (untested!) faith in the attractions of 'liveness' but, at the beginning of the period of popular television in Britain, the producer John Swift was making claims which would be echoed long after the novelty effect of television viewing had been exchanged for social and domestic routine:

> The primary function of television is to transmit pictures as they are being made . . . the *basic* attraction is not so much the subject matter it presents but the realization that whatever is happening *is happening at the time.* (italics in original, Caughie 1991*b*: 32)

The recorded image, sometimes transmitted 'live', could for many years be differentiated from the cinematic image in terms of its size, definition, and colour. Early television worked with a scanning system and limited lines of resolution which gave poor definition and it was restricted to monochrome long after feature cinema had largely shifted to colour (although colour printing had yet to develop in many areas of print publicity and journalism, so the meanings of monochromatic imagery did not have the aesthetic and historical overtones which they carry today). In the late 1990s, television images are often of very high definition, with excellent colour and stability. The comparability with cinema is therefore stronger (a point to which the extensive home video market is testimony). Yet screen size persists as an important distinction between cinematic and televisual image projection (a point brought out very well and influentially in Ellis 1982). Even allowing for the new range of large screen systems, most television is watched on screens which are many times smaller than those of local cinemas and this has important consequences for the aesthetics of the television image and the psycho-social character of its experiencing by viewers. For instance, the facial close-up on television has not the same expressive force as in the cinema nor, at the other end of the scale, does the wide-angle landscape shot. In fact, given the extensive nature of television's non-fictional output and its dependence on different kinds of to-camera presentation, shots in the 'middle-close-up' range have to be used much more frequently across all the genres. The degree of detail which a television image can carry is also affected by its size. For instance, an interior of a room shown on the cinema screen offers much more potential information for the viewing eye than when shown on television, a point that may well affect directorial decisions about, for instance, the organization of the set, the depth of focus, and the length of a shot.

This is not all a matter of loss. Television's scale, when combined with its typically domestic mode of reception (see Chapter 8), and then its forms of spoken address, provides it with the grounds of a relaxed sociality simply unavailable to cinema. Part of this sociality is the sense of the television device as putting home and studio or home and world into temporary co-presence (again, an effect premissed upon the possibility of liveness across distance). In 1956 the American critic Jack Gould noted how:

> Live television . . . bridges the gap instantly and unites the individual at home with the event afar. The viewer has a chance to be in two places at once. Physically, he may be at his own hearthside but intellectually and, above all emotionally, he is at the cameraman's side. (cited in Boddy 1990: 80)

Moreover, a possible mutuality was noted too. Even in the case of drama, Gould noted that 'the player in the studios and the audience at home have an intrinsic awareness of being in each other's presence' (Boddy 1990: 80).

Two characteristics of much television programme discourse are the social form of the relation between studio and home as this is mediated by presenter appearance and speech (e.g. 'Good evening', 'Welcome', 'That's all for today') and the form of the relation to the 'world', in the news, in holiday series, in sports programmes, etc., as this is also mediated (e.g. 'Our correspondent in Brazil sends this report', 'Now over to Bristol where the South West team is waiting', 'So we went over to New York to have a look', 'At Kempton, the racing has just finished and we're going over to join . . .', 'Now, back to the studio'). A system of movements and returns of this kind, working within programmes as well as down schedules, has implications for the television image as it opens out on to variously socialized spaces from the implicit, and often acknowledged, viewing position of home. Charlotte Brunsdon and David Morley (1978) give a careful analysis of these kinds of modes of address and shifts of visual space in relation to the evening news magazine programme *Nationwide* (BBC), itself grounded in ideas about nation, region, studio, and home and the rapid and smooth transportation between them. Proliferating in their availability via satellite and cable systems, such accessed spaces—fictional and factual, location and studio— accommodate, invite, and guide the domestic view. Although they may differ radically in format and content, their links with home space are often explicitly marked (most obviously and directly in those programmes whose own studio space mimics features of the home in design and furnishing). This gives the typical images-spaces of television a very different character from those of cinema.

The Moving Image

Television provides us with a moving image but, more fundamentally, it provides us with an imaging which has a time dimension as part of its expressive capacity. For periods, this can work effectively when the image does not move (both when the shot itself remains static and/or when nothing within the shot moves). But kinetic appeal, the promise and pleasure of watching movement and action, is an important part of television, both in factual and fictional programmes. More broadly, narrative (see Chapter 5) is a major organizing principle of television, the capacity to show physical action and also to indicate physical causality and chronology are central to its cultural identity.

In his seminal comparison of television and cinema, John Ellis (1982) sought to distinguish between the more fluid, dynamic organization of cinematic image sequences and the segmental character of television; the latter a consequence of particular production conventions and the requirements of the television economy for a regular and extensive supply of programmes. This made for a depictive practice which used real-time sequences extensively, did not jump locations as frequently as in film, and, across a number of genres and formats, relied on a segment of several minutes duration rather than a shot as its basic unit (so, for instance, a dramatic scene typically stayed for some time within a particular interior, showing a lengthy exchange of dialogue, before a shift of setting). Ellis's account picked up on a real depictive distinction but probably tended to give it sharper outlines than it actually had (this is partly a problem of essentializing across the whole of television, where the sheer range of forms and functions is potentially treacherous). Certainly, the advancement of production technology since the 1980s, combined with the increase in the number of depictive options employed and the mobility of their combination, makes clear formal distinctions much harder to maintain today. However, the fact that cinema is primarily fiction based whilst television, internationally, includes a wide variety of non-fictional images continues to make the general visual profile of the two media very different.

The question of television's 'realism' is at one level an issue to do with the primary properties of the television moving image—its rendering, through a recording, of the appearances and action of the real world. Television's apparent ability to provide visible evidence instantaneously might be seen to confer a realist character to its reportage. But reportage offers to be a direct account of the real, explicit in the visual claims it makes about the status of what and who we are seeing. These claims may be open to debate but this is not usually a matter of how *like* the real the news appears. In fact, in television study the term 'realism' has mostly been applied to visual and narrative aspects of fiction where, following the usage in literary and film studies, it indicates a 'real-seeming' effect achieved by directorial design. Even expressions like 'documentary realism' are mostly used to indicate, not the evidential qualities of primary depiction (e.g. an image sequence of a ship going aground upon rocks in relation to the specific reality of this event) but the way in which these qualities are deployed according to rules—including those of narrative continuity, chronology, and space—derived from fiction. However, as these comments might suggest, realism is a confusing notion indicating a number of ways in which a moving image might gain a heightened semblance to the real or even somehow be certified by reality. Seemingly indispensable, it has often clouded rather than clarified analysis, a point developed later in the book.

The moving image, of course, whether factual or fictional in derivation, almost always and quite quickly becomes the edited image.

The Edited Image

Action—images of movement—can be caught within the single shot and displayed as such (a domestic camcorder scene of children playing on a beach might be of this kind, although even the area of amateur production has become increasingly ambitious in its portrayals). Television studios can also edit 'in-channel', mixing the output from several cameras in different positions and perhaps in different locations to produce a multi-shot image sequence which can be transmitted live or taped for later broadcasting. But the post-production electronic editing of videotape (having attained a precision rivalling that of the physical editing of film) provides television with its characteristic modes of recorded depiction, its movements of view and rhythms of seeing, its matching of sound to image.

These differ from its characteristic modes of 'live' portrayal, which often combine voiced-over commentary, shots of extended duration, and in-channel cuts which display sharp perceptual disjunctions and unsteady movement of the camera in the attempt to follow action. Early Outside Broadcast transmissions privileged their actuality and immediacy values, even though the technology necessitated a certain level of rehearsal for many ostensibly spontaneous sequences and a careful plan of camera switching to ensure an acceptable level of visual coherence across transitions. In the 1990s, a more ambitious sense of the spontaneous informs much of television practice, backed up by a radically improved lightweight camera technology. The newer breakfast shows, for instance, largely following developments in 'youth' programming, have self-consciously refashioned the live aesthetic in the direction of new levels of unpredictability and energy in the movement and the disruption of the visual field. The camera pursues people running down corridors, 'whip pans' to pick out unsuspecting members of the live audience, is worn by participants in an outdoor game to provide intercut point-of-view shots, appears to be going up the nose of the presenter, and so on (Lury forthcoming considers the terms of this refashioning, drawing on several generic examples). However, the aesthetic is still one which grounds its viewer appeal in the specific content of the image, read as a co-presented action or circumstance.

Editing techniques and styles have received close attention by critics and researchers, building on the critical attention which has been given to editing in film. Not surprisingly, it is post-production editing rather than in-channel editing which has had most scrutiny, being both more considered, more complex, and involving a deeper level of perceptual management than live editing is usually able to accomplish. Editing moves the viewer across times and places, it involves a continual process of opening up and then closing down specific looks at the world, which may, for instance, be a studio world, a dramatic world, or the evidential and expository world of a documentary programme. Edits connect spaces and times, themes and moods, working to regulate the sense we make of images by providing us with a changing visual context for their interpretation, setting up lines of anticipation and prompting retrospective assessment (the image we are seeing in relation to the ones we shall see and the ones we have seen—see the account of perception and editing in Messaris 1994). Both in fiction and non-fiction, they provide perceptual and thematic separations and continuities, they generate narrative development and discursive progress (a function discussed further in Chapters 5 and 10). We are, as viewers, carried through their breaks and linkages into the overall coherence of, for instance, a major scene unfolding in a hospital drama, a programme on the history of beer, a news report on loans for university students.

Editing has often been the subject of critical dispute, but the editing of non-fiction raises different problems from the editing of fiction, even though some criticism has worked with a refusal of this generic distinction. As I have noted, fictional editing styles are a key part of the debate about realism. Television, though it certainly has its experimentalists and (in some countries) an avant-garde, does not have the cultural profile which has allowed film-makers to develop their work in strong relation to concurrent developments in the visual arts, drama, and literature. It is pre-eminently a popular form, placing emphasis on accessibility as a result both of its public and its commercial remit. Its management of narrative space and time, its distinctive modes of storytelling, have been criticized as producing too neatly self-contained a rendering of the world, a world of self-evident truths and neat illustrations.

In non-fiction, the argument has sometimes focused on that proximity to the coherence of fictional worlds which many documentary and news feature items display, mixing observationalist and dramatic methods of shooting and editing. However, the main debates about non-fiction have largely concentrated on the evidential use of imagery (remarked on earlier but see also my comments on talk and image in Chapter 4) and on its various functions in the support of exposition and argument. Whilst image or image sequences are often used in a directly evidential way in non-fictional programming, particularly news and current affairs (e.g. the Prime Minister arriving, the building under discussion being demolished, the police attacking the crowd), there is also a more extensive use of image sequences in a supportive and illustrative role, where precisely the mode of editing employed in the shift from image to image, sequence to sequence, is crucial. Image sequences may, for example, work in relation to a voice-over of historical commentary, reportage, or interview testimony. The status of what is seen can vary from the directly illustrative (e.g. comment about Hitler's emphasis on national youth movements in the 1930s over a shot of his attendance at a youth rally) to the highly indirect and indicative (e.g. comment about British industrial pollution over shots of Liverpool from a 1920s film about the Cunard shipping line; comment about changing working-class attitudes to health and lifestyle over contemporary shots of Christmas shoppers in a town centre). Archive usage may include material from feature fiction interwoven with actuality sequences. Whatever the means, in producing the movement and flow of the edited television image, a large and diverse image bank may be drawn on, perhaps combined with kinds of 'live' material.

Aesthetic Elements of the Edited Image

Edited images in factual programmes may well encourage a high level of transparency in the viewing relationship. They may cue the spectator, perhaps by voice-over, perhaps by properties of the visualization itself, to invest meanings in the portrayal (of, say, beaches in Spain, of housing estates in Leeds, of police action at a football match) which do not take account of any motivations or selectivity on the part of the image-maker or of the construction process itself. If they cue in this way, however, there is no guarantee that they will succeed in securing such an innocent reading. As I suggest elsewhere (Chapter 8), audience research has raised a number of questions about the cultural and psychological factors which are involved in achieving a transparency effect of this kind or, by contrast, in producing a critical and sceptical response. On the other hand, a programme may have an interest in encouraging pleasure in its own depictive devices—zooms, inserts, camera movements, and types of edit serving to project the flow of the television image as openly, pleasingly, and skilfully artefactual. Many newer kinds of programme in the British schedules have adopted this openly crafted style and, in his book *Televisuality* (1995), John Caldwell sees such videographic density as comprising what is fast becoming a marked aesthetic in American programming of all kinds.

Before looking at elements of the edited image in a little more detail, it may be useful to note again how it has been the factual rather than the fictional image which has been the subject of the most intensive attention in television research. The medium's range of non-fictional genres, particularly its journalistic modes, has provoked a level of enquiry about the origins and organization of the image and its truth relations which for obvious reasons is not applicable to fictional material. Of course, fiction poses other kinds of question about the use of the image in the telling of stories, the portrayal of setting and character, and the generation of knowledge and pleasure.

I want to proceed by looking briefly at three components of television's edited image—framing and composition, *mise-en-scène*, and figuration.

■ **Framing and composition**

With the exception of films designed initially or concurrently for cinema release, television images are framed and composed with the factors of reduced screen size and domestic contexts of reception in mind. The naturalistic 'location' aesthetics of news, current affairs, and some kinds of documentary programmes encourage a raw look, with material displaying a spontaneity of visualization complementary to what are often strongly projected modes of direct address speech in voice-over or in vision. The image is framed and composed reactively, the world turned into shot within depictive protocols which require comprehensibility (focus, spatial positioning, figure/background relations, indicators of size and distance, etc.) but which would only be compromised by a more considered artefactual appearance, even assuming that production conditions allowed this.

Studio programmes of all kinds are often anchored in speech, in vision or in voice-over. The result is often a visualization which serves primarily to indicate the space and place of talk (see Chapter 4). When the image itself becomes more prominent, it may be prone to the kind of hyperactivity which Caldwell notes in recent American programming, developing a rhythm of frame-breaking, superimposition, and computer-assisted manipulation (as in a game show or a breakfast chat show) although still basing itself on a regular return to in-vision speech. The image use of television commercials and of some pop video work has contributed substantially to the visual repertoire of small screen/home viewing possibilities, with their parameters of scale, visual field, and intimacy. In popular television series drama, the extensive use of close-up and medium close-up provides for the special kinds of character familiarity, proximity, and everydayness which these fictions seek to generate in exploring dimensions of the domestic and the social.

■ Mise-en-scène

Mise-en-scène describes the 'staging' of what appears in the frame—its lighting, its settings, and the behaviour of those depicted in so far as this is within the control of the director. As noted above, the distinctive sociality of television and the fact that popular television includes a wide range of non-fiction forms means that the social and narrative spaces upon which television opens up often carry a stronger sense of the naturalistic and the mundane than those of the cinema. In Britain, the realist commitments of various types of reportage have combined with the thematic and formal realism of the soaps (with their dominant focus on working-class living) to produce an aesthetics of the everyday: television either showing, or somehow responding to, 'ordinary' life as it unfolds, messily and casually, in the daily sequence of work, recreation, and relationships and the interplay of the planned with the accidental, the significant with the merely circumstantial. This is an aesthetics the empirical and conservative tendencies of which have so far largely withstood generic innovation towards more busy and fantastic forms. Although by definition a major component of drama, mise-en-scène is an important aspect of factual programming too, especially of those forms which are allowed greater scope to aestheticize the rendered world, to style the real more thoroughly than the normative conventions of reportage permit. For instance, many types of documentary attempt extensively to stage and direct the referent of their images (setting, action, and persons as appropriate) in order to heighten illustrative force and viewing pleasure (see Corner 1996a on the diverse procedures which have been employed here).

Television also, routinely, opens up on the space of the 'show'—the entertaining studio event which may often be set in theatre-like circumstances, with a live audience responding to staged performance. Game shows, quiz shows, talk shows, studio debate programmes, youth magazine programmes, music programmes, and variety specials all variously employ this form. The work of mise-en-scène here is not to access a space of naturalistic action but to access a space of stimulating artifice, a theatre (perhaps literally so) for contrived eventuality and self-conscious performance. The development of studio set design and programme direction to this end (spaces for entrances and exits, spaces for action and for interaction, relations of live audience to performance, depth of focus and focal shifts) is attracting more attention in international television studies. This is a broad television mode which, in its three-dimensionality, can be contrasted with the two-dimensional video-graphic density pointed to by Caldwell, although many new formats display innovations in the combining of both, thus appealing to a new generation of viewers.

■ **Figuration**   By figuration I mean to describe the capacity of the image to generate associative resonance beyond literal depiction. Cinema, and then within this the forms of self-consciously 'art cinema', have explored the symbolic properties of the image most extensively. Television is a popular medium and sustained and/or dense associative imaging is often regarded as 'difficult', annoying the audience with problems of comprehensibility and breaking the dominant mood of the relaxed and the casual. However, across a great range of its programming, television employs a secondary symbolism to generate significance above the level of primary depiction, whether this depiction occurs in reportage, drama, or studio entertainment. Programme title sequences often show this capacity at its most condensed (seeking to convey the essence of a programme's identity through an associative strategy of imagery, sound, and music) but more intermittent and indirect figuration occurs routinely across most genres. Sometimes it is generated upwards from, and has pertinence for, the literal depiction (e.g. the sustained close-up on an object to give it symbolic emphasis). Within news and documentary programming, image-produced associations of this kind can be regarded by viewers as implicit propositions, a form of directorial commentary which then can be the subject of controversy and charges of 'bias'. For instance, a brief shot of wind-blown litter in a sequence about the restoration of Liverpool's public parks might be regarded as saying something about the dirtiness of the city (on the issues surrounding the biased image, see Philo 1990). Elsewhere, associative imaging operates on a plane of metaphoric suggestiveness (either propositional or primarily aesthetic) at some distance from any primary depictive function. Here again, developments in advertising and in popular music video have traded in clichéd cultural codings as well as in novelty and originality—red balloons float in blue skies, surf breaks on beaches, the earth is seen from space, cars are trapped in an urban traffic jam.

A final point to note in consideration of the edited image is the differential effect of the modes of edit themselves in organizing meaning and regulating viewers' engagement with programmes. Cuts, wipes, dissolves, and fades all operate with different indications, if sometimes only subtly so, as to the relation between the shots which they connect. For instance, the cut carries the potential to deliver a perceptual shock (perhaps of a direct contrast or of the utterly unexpected) and to advance narrative in ways which the quieter linkage achieved by dissolves and fades does not. The continuities and disjunctions across space and time which television has wanted to achieve in its depictive work have often turned on the modes of edit employed from the technological options available. The political and cultural character of the particular ways of seeing which television has endorsed has thus also depended in part on this level of articulation of the image (see the useful discussion in Caughie 1991*b*).

Images, Viewing, and Viewers

I noted earlier that television's imagery has been seen as a principal constituent of a 'society of the image', in which relations of mediated looking have displaced those of reading and listening. The consequences of this are, I suggested, nearly always judged to be negative ones—the displacement of substance by appearance, the corruption of knowledge values by the merely diverting, the distortion of moral values by an excess of superficial, vicarious experience and by the kinds of suspect foci for imaginative identification provided on the screen. Frequently, in a range of academic writing and journalism, politics is seen to have become irretrievably cosmetic as a result of its increased dependence on images of politicians, often projecting them both as ordinary and as stars in strategically inconsistent portrayal, rather than the development and discussion of political ideas (see, for instance, Franklin 1994).

Most of this criticism is inclined to ignore the true extent and the continuing importance of the non-televisual in society, including within contemporary politics, but assessment of the changes encouraged by electronic imagery has produced a strand of thoughtful and provocative commentary which is likely to continue.

In an early American paper on 'The Phantom World of TV', written in 1956, the writer Gunther Anders noted several characteristics of the 'image world' of television. He advanced the following four speculative propositions:

Since the world comes to us only as an image, it is half-present and half-absent, in other words, phantom-like; and we too are like phantoms . . .

When the world is perceivable, but no more than that, i.e. not subject to our action, we are transformed into eavesdroppers and Peeping Toms.

When an event that occurs at a definite place is broadcast, and when it can be made to appear at any other place as a 'broadcast', it becomes a movable, indeed almost ubiquitous object, and has forfeited its spatial location, its *principium individuationis*.

When the actual event is socially important only in its reproduced form, i.e. as a spectacle, the difference between being and experience, between reality and image of reality, is abolished. (Anders 1956: 363)

These formulations contain some questionable phrasings but it is surprising how much they prefigure the kinds of critique of the image which emerges in the postmodernist writing of the 1980s (classically, in Baudrillard 1988). The emphasis on spatial dislocation, spectacularity, and 'phantom' presence is particularly relevant here. There is, in both cases, an apocalyptic tone excluding consideration of the modifying or even conflicting possibilities and instances which a more sociological approach would want to register. But the rapid change in the scale and intensity of image culture is still insufficiently recognized and the value of this kind of commentary lies in its attempt imaginatively to grasp those deeper changes which, as yet, many more sober accounts are unwilling to consider.

In their influential 1977 study of how one television documentary operated as a textual system, Stephen Heath and Gillian Skirrow identify distinctive properties of the image and the viewing relations which follow. Their assessment is made largely in terms which I have reviewed earlier in this chapter:

> In one sense, the television image is effectively 'live', very different from that of film. Where the latter depends on the immobility of the frame, the former, electronic and not photographic, is an image in perpetual motion, the movement of a continually scanning beam, whatever the status of the material transmitted, *the image as a series of electric impulses is necessarily 'as it happens'* . . . the cinema screen film image is distant, inaccessible, fascinatingly fixed (all the references to fetishism in film criticism and theory); the television image is close (the television field occupying a much reduced part of the spectator's visual field), available (the TV set a controllable possession), interpellative . . . (Heath and Skirrow 1977: 53, italics added)

They go on to note that:

> The immediate time of the image is pulled into a confusion with the time of the events shown, tending to diminish the impression of the mode of presence in absence characteristic of film, suggesting a permanently alive view on the world, the generalised fantasy of the television institution of the image that it is *direct*, and direct *for me*. (Heath and Skirrow 1977: 53–4, italics in original)

The extent to which the actual mode of constitution of the television image contributes to a liveness effect independent of specific representational content seems to be highly questionable. Moreover the liveness of television, however technologically grounded, is essentially a matter of generic formulae, depictive conventions, and modes of address. But the difference between television's collapsing of time frames and cinema's strong sense of 'presence in absence' is, I think, an instructive one. Elsewhere in this book (see Chapter 5) I explore further the question of television's times and the often complex structures of temporality which programmes can have.

In a much more recent article, Kevin Robins and Les Levidow (1991) look at how aspects of the Gulf War were televised and particularly at how the imaging of the war brought viewers into a vicarious relationship with combat. They are most concerned with the use of video footage from weapon systems themselves, 'target videos' showing the moment of impact and placing the viewer in a relationship to action which replicates aspects of video-gaming (hence, the use of the term 'Nintendo effect' in general debate about the ethics of this visual usage). The authors describe the nature of the new image space:

> In the Gulf War, the vision of the long camera shot extended the moral distanciation of previous wars. The silent movie filmed from the bomb bay or from the nose of the missile had a similar numbing remoteness. In this war, however, the rationalization of vision was pushed further. Here we had an apparently greater visual proximity between the killer and the victim. Indeed, the missile-nose view of the target simulated a super-real closeness which no human being could ever attain. It was the

ultimate voyeurism . . . Seeing was split off from feeling. (Robins and
Levidow 1991: 325)

They conclude in the most general of terms:

Thus Desert Storm has highlighted what is potentially dehumanizing
about the role of images in our society, in our culture of viewing.
Through our vision technologies we were able to disavow the reality.
(Robins and Levidow 1991: 327)

There is no doubt as to the scopic originality and force of the target-video
footage, carrying the steady development and naturalization of the surveillance image into an utterly new realm and incorporating it within prime-
time news, where it quickly became of significance in the whole depiction of
the war. However, it is more difficult to read the psycho-social relations of
viewing straight from the character of the image. The intermixing between
'serious' and 'play' caused by elements of the news framing on the one
hand and the proximity to gaming on the other is not easily calculated. The
extent to which real ethical concerns survived the potential displacing pull of
such imagery is documented in other studies of the Gulf War (see Morrison
1992). Despite their alertness to new dimensions of the televised image, the
authors remain too uninquisitive about the social processes of interpretation, positing an image which simply *enforces* its meanings upon the viewer.

The Changing Ecology of the Television Image

The kind of pleasure in viewing which television encourages is, for the
reasons discussed earlier, less intense than that associated with cinema. The
opening out of various fictional and non-fictional spaces in relation to home,
the explicitly sociable and often talk-driven character of many programme
formats, the screen ratios in relation to life-size—all work to give the television image a more dispersed character, variously permeating the everyday
more casually than cinematic depiction and engaging a generally less profound psychodynamic response at the level of the image itself. I shall explore
this more in Chapters 9 and 10, where I look at the questions of pleasure and
knowledge posed by television.

I want to finish this chapter with a note about the new ecology of the
television image which is slowly becoming established in Britain, and is at
various stages of development internationally. This is part of the broader,
complex changes in television's character which are reviewed in Chapter 11.
Perhaps the most important component of this new image order is multi-
channel competition, which increases the requirement of programmes both
initially to attract and then to retain viewers in a situation where a range
of alternatives is easily available. It seems to me that the most obvious response to this situation is a quickened tempo of programme development,
with an increasing need for regular high spots (sub-narrative climax points,
visual 'treats', etc., event resolutions) and the time available between high
spots being subsequently reduced. Across many of its dimensions, the image
may become busier, indeed in some programmes frenetic, complementing a
more exclamatory style of spoken address. New technologies of digital image

production and editing will also allow a much more thoroughly worked and animated image to be employed. Distortions, superimpositions, multi-image framing, and a high mobility of the image within screen space will result, together with new kinds of fabrication based on digital sampling and mixing. Within certain programme formats, the interface with the presentational modes of the internet and of CD ROM display is already apparent. Caldwell (1995) discerns four different modes at work—the painterly, the plastic, the transparent, and intermedia (1995: 151 provides a tabulation). Each one employs a different approach to electronic post-production, effecting transformations and/or deformations of textures, perspectives, planes, and framings which are not so much stylistic elaborations as fundamental changes in the ontology of the image. Perhaps his most important point here is the suggestion that new trends in television do not depend upon either the 'reality effect' or the 'fiction effect' for their success but upon the 'picture effect' (1995: 152). This involves '*the television image itself consuming television images*' (1995: 147, italics in original). Despite this increasing reflexivity in the kind of picturing it offers, however, it is likely that the representational, referential axis of television, variously deployed, will continue to be primary across most of the generic range, albeit in ways which produce new constituents of the image, new image combinations, and new kinds of depictive significance.

Although it has its own specificity as a topic for analysis, the television image is necessarily implicated in most, if not all, research, commentary, and argument about the nature and function of the medium. Further engagement with its many aspects and their consequences will therefore be found at points throughout my other chapters.

4

Talk

TALK of various kinds is, of course, an element of most television. It is not surprising that it extensively drew on, and has since variously shadowed, developments in radio. Although its many distinctive capacities for producing and combining images constitute television's most direct way of engaging, and appealing to, audiences it is through speech that television addresses its viewers and holds them in particular relations both to specific programmes and to channel and station identities. Talk thus generates the socio-communicative sphere within which televisions images operate. Quite quickly in the development of British radio in the 1920s (see Scannell and Cardiff 1991), a range of informal, familial registers for presentation existed alongside the more distanced, official phrasings and tones which had, in part, derived from the pre-radio traditions of public speaking. Sir John Reith, the BBC's first Director-General, had been enthusiastic about the maintenance, albeit through adaptation, of earlier styles of spoken address and the kinds of authority, deference, and forms of politeness which they reproduced. But the generic range of radio entertainment immediately required presentational forms which extended beyond the scope of earlier public talk. The novel element of addressing individual listeners, or very small groups of them, in their own homes clearly suggested the need for new rhetorical conventions too. Radio required a different performance from speakers—earlier skills of the theatre, the public platform, the classroom, etc., might be useful but a direct application was rarely possible. In the development of American radio services, a more colloquial approach was, from the start, the consequence of commercially financed services and the need to treat the listener as a potential customer as well as (and sometimes rather than) a citizen within a national, political, and cultural collectivity.

In addition to the forms of direct speech, addressed to the listener, radio pioneered indirect uses of speech too, quite apart from the emergence of a dramatic dialogue distinctive to the medium. Of these forms, the live or recorded interview, an indirect form which is really only a direct form pretending not to be, has become a staple broadcast speech convention. It is no exaggeration to say that the broadcast interview, particularly the television interview, is now one of the most widely used and extensively developed formats for public communication in the world. When the conventions of sound broadcasting were incorporated into a medium which allowed a fuller projection of personality, of meaning and feeling (through facial expression and gesture), and often of context too, the social relations of the interview became defining not just for contemporary broadcasting but for contemporary culture and politics.

In this chapter I want to look at how questions of talk figure in the analysis of television. As in other chapters, this requires an engagement both with features of television itself and with features of enquiry and criticism. In fact, the last few years have seen an upsurge of academic interest in forms of televised talk. There are two reasons for this. First of all, work in applied linguistics has become interested in media language with the result that a literature of closely focused analysis has emerged, going well beyond the often rather selective and sketchy treatments of speech in most mainstream media research. As well as its interest in technical questions of language deployment, this literature has often had an interest in social relations and power (an interest often signalled by the use in studies of the broader and more socio-political term 'discourse' instead of 'language'). The second reason for the upsurge of interest is the way in which recent generic innovation in television has often developed around more relaxed, franker, and revelatory kinds of speech. The new talk-show formats, ranging from the shows inserted into daytime schedules to the big prime-time series with celebrity guests, have perhaps attracted more attention in recent international debate than any other form, with the possible exception of soap opera.

An example of the first tendency, attention from applied linguistics, would be the interest stimulated by the publication of Norman Fairclough's *Media Discourse* (1995), although Scannell (1991) provided a pioneering precedent for the combination of linguistic detail and historical and sociological enquiry. An example of a British response to the second tendency would be Livingstone and Lunt's *Talk on Television* (1994), a book which situates aspects of the new talk show in an interdisciplinary perspective, looking at performance, at viewer reception, and at political and public functions.

I want to explore current issues in the study of television talk, including conceptual disputes, at a later stage in this chapter. However, a good sense of the special social character of broadcast speech, of the kinds of imaginative and affective relations it generates and sustains, can be got from a brilliantly perceptive paper first published over forty years ago, in 1956. Given its qualities, it is not surprising that Donald Horton's and R. Richard Wohl's observations on 'Mass Communication as Para-Social Interaction' (1956) has been much cited in the recent crop of studies.

Horton and Wohl subtitle their study, 'Observations on Intimacy at a Distance'. Their focus is on how the illusion of face-to-face relationship is achieved in broadcasting and what the consequences might be, psychological and social, of having a public realm extensively mediated in terms of this illusion. How are identity and relationship managed in these circumstances? More specifically, how are the bonds of sociability established, a sociability which bears a resemblance to that of primary social groups and which relies upon listeners or viewers playing a psychologically active role? In the context of 1990s research it is interesting that the authors see one of the main implications of their work as being a radical questioning of assumptions about viewers being passive in relation to broadcast material, a debate which has never gone away in television studies despite radical changes in its terms (and continuing imprecision about what passivity, and by implication activity, might mean in this context). Under a sequence of subheadings, the paper explores a number of conventions of performance then in use by broadcasting personalities. The authors draw into their discussion of the para-social not only entertainment programmes but the characters of popular dramatic fiction. This makes their account even more broadly perceptive, extending into the changing terms and social relations of the popular imagination brought about by broadcasting.

What implications for personal, political, and cultural life do the authors draw from their survey of para-social practice? As in so many studies which would follow, there is a measure of ambivalence here. The artefactual, 'false' character of the social relations being projected is certainly registered. However, a principal point of emphasis is the lack of a sharp differentiation, in everyday experience, between the para-social encounters of broadcasting and 'the network of actual social relations'. Here, the authors' account touches on a theme which, in different aspects, regularly appears throughout the present book—the interpenetration, blurring, or collapse of the boundaries between public and private realms. Horton and Wohl not only want to argue for the activity of the audience in constructing the new forms of relationship, against those who would stress passive roles, they also want to argue for the integration of mediated relationships into ordinary life against those who would stress only fantasy or dream perspectives. The question of the degree of self-awareness, of play, which might be introduced into the formation of these relationships by viewers is, however, not addressed. This leaves the perceived falseness and simulation uneasily close to suggesting a duping, a deception, of the viewers, albeit one aided by their own interpretative and responsive behaviour. The idea that the kinds of virtual relationships we enjoy with television personalities and performers are both an expansion of real sociality and yet also suspect is an ambivalence which runs through current commentary too, if in different terms (see, for instance, my discussion of Meyrowitz's writing in Chapter 10).

In fact, we can contrast the sociological import of their findings with those made three years earlier by Kurt and Gladys Lang in their classic case-study of television's 'unique perspective' (1953). I have remarked on the scope and suggestiveness of this early enquiry into the terms of live event broadcasting in other work (Corner 1995). I would simply want to note here how important commentary speech is to the overall effect which Lang and Lang see as so potentially damaging to the American democratic process. For them, the television commentator acts as a kind of showman, cueing in the viewers to an interpretation of the pictures through speech which is strategically distortive in its descriptions (always seeking to increase magnitude and significance) and constantly celebratory in inclination (with a vested interest in portraying the success of the event).

Although written before Horton and Wohl's paper appeared, the Langs' analysis of commentary essentially connects with para-social relations, particularly the aligning of the experience of television viewers with that of spectators actually present at the event studied (the procession and ceremonies of the civic visit of General MacArthur to Chicago following his return from Asian command). This alignment is primarily an achievement of voiced-over speech, bringing televiewers into a common event realm with ongoing actuality and its emotional dynamics. As in many later studies, it is the personalizing of the public and the political which attracts attention from the researchers. Perceptively, they remark not only on the way in which the viewer at home is brought into participation but also the way in which the terms of the commentary encourage the sense that the live spectators are enjoying the same sustained and personalized focus on the celebrity visitor which television is providing for viewers. Thus a false mutuality is established, which in the researchers' view further acts to confirm the credibility and persuasiveness of television's version of 'what happened'.

Lang and Lang's concern with the transformative function of the descriptions spoken across the televised pictures has been echoed in much subsequent research into live event broadcasting, including both that of state ceremonies and of sporting occasions (Dayan and Katz 1992 is perhaps the most ambitious study to date) as well as being picked up more widely in a range of work on factual television.

I now want to look more closely at the relations between speech and image. As we have already seen, these relations have often been central to discussion of the forms and consequences of television talk.

Speech and Image in Direct and Indirect Address

John Ellis (1982) has brought out well the distinctiveness of television's direct address, whereby viewers are spoken to in a register deriving more from interpersonal than from mass-public communication. Performed in voice-over, this develops the conventions established in broadcast radio, with the added, modifying factor that the speech relates, with various degrees of directness, to images. The images retain their autonomy as a significatory strand requiring interpretation, but the standard practice in television is for the talk to regulate this interpretation, even though the images also exert an effect on the interpretation of the talk. One reason for this is that speech can be descriptively specific (e.g. names, dates, places, states, and conditions) in a way that the pictures cannot. So we can quickly imagine a travel programme, a cookery programme, a sports broadcast, a social documentary, a news report, or indeed an advertisement in which voiced-over speech had this primary role. But televised direct address can also be in vision. In this mode, the conventions of speech are joined by conventions of 'look'; the speaker engages the hearer in simulated eye-contact via the camera lens and, with variations as to formality, displays the facial behaviours associated with interpersonal exchange. The increased bonding achieved by this form of speech was one of the factors noted by Horton and Wohl in their study. More recent commentators (see, for instance, Morse 1985; Tolson 1985) have regarded direct address, in-vision speech to be television's most powerful discursive mode, generating a form of viewing relationship and a disposition to the institution of television which place it right at the centre of the medium's symbolic and ideological identity.

Television has now developed a large repertoire of styles for in-vision direct address, many of them allowing for the degree of individuation which success as a presenter/performer (with its distinctions of persona) requires. The speech/appearance combination for location journalism does not offer the same scope for innovation and idiosyncrasy as that for stand-up comedy, certainly, but even here the possible repertoire for making para-social contact with the viewer has increased (for instance, the new relaxed sociability of breakfast show reports, or the manic styling of youth magazine reportage). Among current presenter types on television, the game-show host is perhaps charged with the task of producing the most vivaciously personal and yet managerially ambitious performance. The host uses speech and facial display to project a performance of distinctive individual qualities (usually including comic talent) and at the same time to control both the real social relations with the contestants and the live audience and also the para-social relations with viewers (through direct address to camera and use of close-up). Display and control dimensions need to be kept in strategic balance, which will vary according to the complexity of programme business and the kind of social atmosphere which is sought.

I noted that voiced-over direct address speech sets up communicative relations with the viewer but also refers to the images, thus producing a kind of triangle of relations—speech/viewer; image/viewer; speech/image. The speech/image relations in this mode can be very direct, as when the speaker looks at the image with us, opening up the meanings we are to find in it. Instances of this could be taken from a variety of programmes, including the news, but the use of the still image of a painting in a sequence of spoken art criticism would be a sharper illustration. Such relations can also be highly indirect, as when, say, in a history programme, the speech offers a complex and abstract argument about diplomatic relationships whilst the images draw on archive materials to provide a visualization (say, of city streets) with little direct informational yield, perhaps merely a point of engagement for the eye during this passage.

If the problem with in-vision direct address has frequently been seen to lie in the communicative bonding it establishes with the viewer, potentially replacing a proper critical distance with para-social familiarity, the problem with voice-over direct address has often been viewed as that of self confirmation. In this process, the accompanying images are read *both* in alignment with what is said *and* as independent verification of its truth. Clearly, it is only when the speech and the image have a good degree of local fit that an effect of this sort can occur. The image has to be initially readable as evidence for propositions, implicit or explicit, on the soundtrack. However, the business of co-attending to speech and images makes it quite possible for a viewer to blur what is heard and seen. Propaganda and advertising often work with this strategy. For instance, there is the (apocryphal?) instance of the First World War Allied propaganda film which purported to show the extremity of the German economy and German standards of living by an actuality sequence showing a sausage factory where sawdust was being added to the meat mix to give extra food volume! The monochrome visuals merely showed various ingredients; it was the commentary which mentioned sawdust. But, so the story goes, many people reported having seen the sawdust, giving the material a far stronger credibility than a verbal report.

Such an example from propaganda history is complicated by the factor of willingness to believe, but the way in which visible evidence on television is often only fully realized as such by descriptive and propositional elements in its speech accompaniment is an important dimension of how television attains meaning. Direct address voice-over speech works routinely, in a wide range of genres and formats, across image sequences spanning different spaces and employing images at different points on the spectrum between the literal and the figurative (see my discussion of this latter distinction in Chapter 3). The kinds of circularity of proof which can result often put extreme pressure on the integrity of production practice. Partly as a consequence of this, there has been a strong move away from the use of commentary voice in much mainstream documentary television, preference being given instead to interview speech and overheard speech (a mode initially distinctive to the naturalism of observational documentary but one which is now employed more widely in popular factual programming).

Direct address speech is a defining feature of television discourse but there are also many forms of indirect address contributing to the social, informational, and entertaining dynamics of television. With few exceptions, indirect address is read *within* the image rather than as a commentary *upon* it. It therefore lacks the regulating externality which the other mode frequently displays. In the various interview formats (location and studio, live and recorded) contemporary television achieves some of its most informatively rich and emotionally powerful sequences of speech. But it also achieves a colloquiality and a vigour of non-professional expression which are important elements in the constitution of television's social identity. Interviews are managed indirect address, in contrast to the unmanaged indirectness of overheard speech in observational formats. Of course, the levels of the management may vary considerably in both cases (for instance, between fully rehearsing interview answers and simply recording spontaneous responses; between setting some of the terms for the conduct of the action to be 'observed' and just recording it without intervention, which is not to say, of course, that it will be unmodified by awareness of the camera's and microphone's presence). Nevertheless, some distinction of the kind I have indicated seems useful and I want to look more closely at the special usage and forms of para-sociality which dialogic speech has produced.

Dialogic Speech as Television Event

The kind of talk designed for overhearing which is produced by interviews has rightly been the object of analytic attention both by media researchers and linguists. Interviews vary in form across a number of options, including live/recorded; location/studio; interviewer in shot/interviewer unseen; questions heard/questions removed. Each option produces a rather different communicative event but the underlying advantages of interviewing remain relatively constant. Among these are the possibilities for questioning it provides, its direct accessing of testimony and viewpoints, and the more relaxed, personable styles of speaking it allows. One can usefully distinguish between three broad types of interview content—information, viewpoint, and experience—even though in practice there is often some overlap between them.

■ Information interviews

These primarily draw on kinds of expertise (e.g. economic, medical, educational, scientific) or direct knowledge of specific events (eyewitnesses, police, and industrial spokespersons, etc.). They may often occur as a short clip lasting only a few seconds and consisting of a single utterance. In a more expansive location style, as employed in news features, documentaries, and a variety of factual series (e.g. holiday programmes, consumer affairs magazines, cookery shows), they may contain a sequence of exchanges and be given a visual framing which projects them as a social episode (see Corner 1996a)—interviewer and interviewee greeting one another and having their speech framed within a particular social space and time (the embassy garden; the dockside cafe; the busy factory floor, etc.).

■ **Viewpoint interviews** While these can occur in different formats and involve speakers of varying status they importantly include those interviews which feature live or recorded interchange with official and, often, élite figures. Viewpoint interviews may be limited in duration, but they frequently contain a number of interviewee utterances and, especially in the case of the political interview, they often develop a conflictual character as the interviewee responds to critically inflected questions and follow-ups. This type of interview has been seen as an important feature of television's democratic role, providing a degree of political accountability, albeit on the media's terms, despite continuing arguments about the evasiveness of politicians and the level of complicity of broadcasters. Not surprisingly, élite political interviews usually involve strategic, relatively impersonal registers—with a focus on point-making tactics and carefully rehearsed description and evaluation. Set up in part as a contest, they often maintain a high level of tension, apparent in the management of the relationship between speakers. Live interviews can develop this theatrical aspect more strongly and engagingly, with the control of the speech and of speaking relationships being done within the interview itself rather than performed upon it later by editing.

■ **Experiential interviews** These have increased in frequency across all formats in recent years. A major contributing factor here has been the development of a whole new range of talk shows in which either celebrities or, in a different format, ordinary people, are given speech opportunities (are variously cued to talk) within a studio setting. However, many documentaries, current affairs, and news programmes have recently intensified their interest in 'experience' of all kinds, linking interview speech to a number of political, social, psychological, and oral-historical projects. Typically, questioning in the experiential interview takes on more of the aspect of counselling than of interrogation. Interview utterance is grounded far more in personal identity than is the case either in informational or viewpoint interviews and the business of description involves acts of personal recollection, sometimes a kind of remembering aloud. Where the memories are traumatic ones (e.g. of social upheaval, personal violence, accidents, and illnesses) the viewing experience can also become shocking and potentially distressing. This type of interviewing has been one of the key areas of development in television over the last decade, bringing both admiration for honesty and depth as well as rebuke for sensationalism and invasion of privacy.

At the end of this chapter, I shall return to the question of what directions the character of interview talk might take in the future. What is clear is that it will remain the communicative core around which a number of very different programme formats are organized, accessing the viewer to personally mediated knowledge and experience and providing kinds of talk forms which augment those of the professional broadcaster. It is noticeable that its use has increased in sports reporting, where, for instance, pre-match, interval, and end-of-game interviews (including those with participants) regularly open up an interior perspective on the unfolding events, complementary to the exterior reading offered by professional commentators. This has been carried forward to become a key ingredient, for instance, of games-based spectaculars and a wide range of game shows aimed at the youth market. In these programmes, the pre- and post-event interview has become an element of talk used less for its value in communicating participants' thoughts and feelings than for the way in which it provides a regular if brief concentration on *person* (celebrity player or ordinary contestant) in what is otherwise an apersonal event. It thus regulates proximity relationships, compensating for the spectator distancing which the programme formats might otherwise produce.

■ **Studio-event exchanges**

I also want to include reference here to what might be regarded as a sub-category of interviewing. This is the studio-event exchange. Quiz shows and game shows, whether involving celebrities or ordinary people, clearly generate a lot of this kind of talk. It differs from the range of interview modes in so far as it is tightly grounded in explicit rules, so that answering is short and directly functional for the event. However, some programmes employing such talk necessarily shift into interview mode at points (conventionally, at the point a participant is introduced, even if elsewhere too). Studio-event exchanges have a strong and distinctive para-social dimension, providing celebrities with performance opportunities and setting up ordinary participants for viewer attention as the focus for empathy but, in some cases, of comic failure too. Talk as an indicator of person and of character is of great importance here, as it slips in and out of the functional and even as it performs the functional. Accent, phrasing, giggling, forms of laughter, expressions of delight and despair, all play a part in creating and sustaining the sociality of the event and of the programme. The forms of studio-event speech now contribute significantly to television as popular culture.

■ **Spontaneous exchange**

Whereas interviews and studio exchanges are designed and managed precisely *to be* overheard, perhaps with phrasings which make this clear (e.g. 'Many viewers, hearing you say that, might well ask . . .; I can assure people in the audience that . . .), there are forms of overheard speech which are much less the product of television design.

Given the emphasis on spontaneity or seeming-spontaneity which is now apparent in the international schedules, overheard speech is becoming more prevalent as a programme ingredient. The accessing of a space of action/speech which is marked as anterior to television's own spaces of performance or of intervention generates distinctive, revelatory qualities. Documentaries in what is often referred to as 'fly-on-the-wall' style have routinely recorded spontaneous overheard speech as part of their generic design, but many other programmes employ it for short observational sequences. Its integrity as independent of television's purposes varies considerably according to the situation being filmed and the programme's more general aims and organization. In some self-conscious usages, it develops a proximity to dramatic dialogue (e.g. certain scenes of occupational interchange—at a hotel reception desk, within a police car, in a teachers' staff room). Within the newer, personalized 'docu-soaps' (in Britain, the BBC's *Hotel* (1997) and *The Cruise* (1998) would be good, recent examples), subjects filmed as ostensibly thinking aloud are often involved in a form of implicit but calculated direct address to film crew and viewer just as their physical behaviour often adapts extensively to the requirements of visual performance.

Although I have primarily been concerned with non-fiction in this chapter, it is important to note the way in which the forms of dramatic speech, in their imitations of spontaneity, not only constitute an important dimension of television talk in themselves but also influence speech found elsewhere in the schedules. Dialogue, perhaps particularly that of popular series drama, plays into viewer perceptions of accents and speech mannerisms as well as perceptions of the articulate, the witty, the dumb, the sentimental, the threatening, and other social categories. It offers a vivacious sense of social type, personal distinctiveness, and emotional circumstance. Comedy programmes often exploit the features of television dialogue in the form of parody. But the growth of reflexivity across the genres has meant that the self-conscious imitation of dramatic speech elements has become a much wider phenomenon, modifying the way in which people choose to be heard speaking on television, particularly in the more entertaining kinds of programme.

Talk and Television Studies: A Concluding Note

Talk, employed in a wide range of registers, is central to the appeal and function of television. Developing from radio, this has contributed to what some have seen as the 'secondary orality' of electronic culture: what now amounts to the privileging of certain kinds of public talk over public writing and public print (see the broader debate on this in Fiske and Hartley 1978). The generic development of television has brought not only an increase in the number of forms of talk which are broadcast, both location and studio based, recorded and live, but it has also in recent years seen a strong shift towards new levels of informality, of spontaneity, of manic performance, of 'bad language', and of licensed rudeness in televised speech.

I remarked earlier that one broad strand of new talk shows—that centred on studio chat with ordinary people—has not merely been innovatory at a formal and thematic level, it has created widespread debate about the nature of television as a public forum and about the way in which forms of talk relate to the political and to the personal. For some commentators, it has shown the possibilities, at least, for a more inclusive, less emotionally repressed public discourse (Livingstone and Lunt 1994; Keane 1995). For others, it represents a suspect erosion of rationality, a championing of feeling over thinking in which a general hostility to expertise harbours a dangerous populism. Certainly, the significance of these new kinds of forum in relation to broader, political questions of decision-making, power, and popular participation remains an issue (see Garnham 1995). Norman Fairclough's ideas about 'conversationalization' nicely capture some of the processes at work in the production of the newer styles of relaxed, dialogical speech, and the uncertainties of assessment which surround them:

> there is a major ambivalence in the case of conversationalization. To put the issue rather baldly, do conversationalized discourse practices manifest a real shift in power relations in favour of ordinary people, or are they to be seen as merely a strategy on the part of those with power to effectively recruit people as audiences and manipulate them socially and politically. (Fairclough 1995: 13)

Fairclough is alert to the ways in which increasing market pressures on programme development are affecting its para-social forms and yet is commendably unwilling to slip into a premature pessimism about all the new modes of mediated 'conversation'.

Livingstone and Lunt engage with the issue by drawing adaptively on the broad theoretical perspective of Habermas (see Chapter 2). Here, the relationships holding between 'system' (the forms of objectified, institutionalized power) and 'life-world' (the realm of experience and subjectivity) are seen to provide the terms upon which the nature and direction of public life in the future will depend. Approvingly, they note how in at least some of the newer kinds of television talk:

> Members of the public are invited to tell their private stories in public, undermining the distinction between private and public in the life-world. Similarly, by holding them accountable, representatives of established power are asked to reveal and examine the relations between policy and professional or commercial interests. (Livingstone and Lunt 1994: 180)

Talk shows, with their mix of storytelling, interrogation, and debate, are thus credited with at least the *capacity* to help transform positively the character and social relations of public speech. Just how much they do this will, in part, be a function of the social aims they set themselves and the assumptions they make about their own relationship with audiences, live and in front of the screen. As Richardson and Meinhof (1999) usefully point out, there are now many different kinds of talk show on American and European television, with a strong representation of the sensational and exhibitionist. Thus, attempts at either a generalized condemnation or a defence may be working with too imprecise an object of argument.

There is no doubt that generic hybridity and new forms of para-social practice will continue to make the nexus between televised talk and the character and norms of public life a matter of concern, echoing some of the issues raised by Horton and Wohl but giving them a more developed political framing. Here, Livingstone and Lunt's approach has advantages over Fairclough's in the attention it pays to the accounts of viewers. For it is clear that, however precise the linguistic analysis, the conditions and consequences of television talk cannot be fully revealed by formal investigation alone. They require to be understood in the meanings attributed by viewers and in the values and dispositions which the medium's performed or overheard versions of social exchange indirectly activate in everyday living.

5
Narrative

THE narrative dimension of television, its various ways of putting stories together through words and images, has attracted a great deal of attention in recent research and even where it has not been the subject of primary interest it has figured as a factor in much commentary about the medium's character and social significance. It is worth noting straight away the difference between discussion of narrative as an aspect of television fiction and discussion of it as an aspect of other television forms, including news and documentary. While in the former case narrative is taken as a prerequisite of programme construction, the focus of analysis and debate then being its precise nature and effects, in the latter case even its very existence has been a matter of dispute and concern, signalling a possible erosion of informational and expository values.

'Narrative' means story-like and since there are a great many ways of telling stories and a number of different components which stories can have, it is not surprising that the application of the term in analysis shows variety and sometimes disagreement. No one would want to argue about the importance of the narrative in, for example, a dramatic series like *Friends* but they may well want to question its importance, or even its existence, in a current-affairs programme.

What are the key components of narrative? Talking primarily of cinema, Bordwell and Thompson (1990: 55) say that 'a narrative is a chain of events in cause-effect relationship occurring in time and space'. It might have been useful to add 'a representation of' at the start of this definition, since narratives are a cultural and discursive phenomenon not properties of real world circumstances and acts. Even then, we have what is only a core definition, one which applies, in part, to discursive forms not primarily appreciated for their narrative value (laboratory reports, for instance, or university lectures). Bordwell and Thompson would readily agree that the chain of events does not have to be chronological, so 'cause-effect' relations may not be linear in their presentation. Of course, it is an important part of fictional plot development precisely to ensure that they are not. Distinctions between the internal elements and mechanisms of narrative are important and I shall return to them later. Before proceeding to look in more detail at how television narrative has been conceptualized and studied I want to put forward two distinctions of my own (though ones doubtless paralelled in the work of others) which I think might be helpful. These are the distinction between spoken narrative and enacted narrative and the distinction between affective and informational narrative functions. Like most distinctions in this book, the second of these is analytic more than substantive and indicates a separation which is sometimes hard to sustain. Despite this, I think the two together catch usefully at issues of importance.

Spoken and Enacted Narrative

Classically, narratives have often been *narrations*, storytelling by a storyteller who takes primary or even exclusive responsibility for the portrayal. In this portrayal, events are described, although they may also be given a degree of enactment too. With the slow and phased transition from oral to literate cultures, written narration, especially in the development of the various forms of the novel, became the pre-eminent form of narration, employing a range of different narrative voices, involving first- and third-person framings. In the eighteenth-century epistolary novel, for instance, readers were addressed directly in an exclamatory style suggestive of a personal letter, thus relating them to the writer and to the story in a manner allowing for intimacy and, frequently, for authorial digressions from the storyline. Eighteenth-century journalism, working with far less of a sense of hard news than is conventional today, also often developed a novelistic narrative approach, expanding on character and incident with considerable authorial leeway. But alongside written narratives, oral storytelling continued as a feature of family and school experience. In the early twentieth century, radio brought about a new orality in public life, in which once again speech performance became culturally primary. The full implications of this are so far underexplored, although Fiske and Hartley, in their *Reading Television* (1978), were right to see television in the context of a new, broadcasting-based, oral tradition and historical work like Scannell and Cardiff's *A Social History of British Broadcasting* (1991) and Scannell's own writings on broadcast language (see, for instance, Scannell 1996) bring out the political and social dimensions of the narrating voice very well indeed. Within television, spoken narratives are to be found in a range of programme genres from, for example, comedy programmes to news bulletins, holiday shows, and specialist interest magazines.

The origins of *enacted* narratives lie in the theatre, and before that in religious ritual. Here, rather than a sequence of acts being described, we are invited to witness them. Immediately, a shift in temporality is evident. However strong in immediacy values its delivery may be, a narrated story is essentially a report on past events. The listener (or reader) imaginatively realizes these events as ongoing action ('then' turned into an imagined 'now') but an action nevertheless framed by the temporal terms of the account, which may shift to 'now' in order to offer commentary on the action, before going back to 'then' in order to describe it further. In enactment, the 'imitation of the action' which Aristotle speaks of in his *Poetics* is presented before us in a relation of co-present observation. Narrational elements may be introduced (various characters speaking to the audience directly from within or outside the action) but the story is primarily told in a physical portrayal. Cinema and then television powerfully supplement and transform the theatrical experience through the various enactments which almost any evening of viewing offers. When Raymond Williams talked of the way in which television had brought about 'a dramatized society' (1974*b*) it was to this important shift in the scale and pervasiveness of enactment that he referred. His comment was partly one about a certain kind of narrativization of society. Of course, television's enacted narratives may well be seen to extend well beyond the vast range of fictional forms, to include those programmes which tell stories with kinds of actuality material, with scenes shot from 'real life'. This question of 'real-life narratives' is a central one in discussion of contemporary television and I shall return to it at points throughout the chapter. I shall also look at the ways in which narration and enactment are combined in many kinds of television, leading to narratives of *mixed* performance.

My second distinction is also related to the categories of the fictional and the factual. The affective dimension of narrative is a matter of the extent to which, and the ways in which, it seeks to create personal involvement, excitement, pleasure, fear, and desire in the viewer. The involvement with narrative is often a para-social one (see Chapter 4), in which engagement with portrayed characters leads to an imaginative investment in their actions and situations. But narratives often have an informational function too, however crude it may seem to call it this. Knowledge, information of different kinds, and perhaps particular viewpoints are being advocated and projected through the instantiations of 'story'. Values are being variously advanced and undercut. This may be done with different degrees of self-consciousness and emphasis. The greater these two are, the more the depiction becomes didactic in character, but arguments about the normative or ideological features of fiction form a major part of theatrical, cinematic, and literary debate.

Where the narrative form is used to shape materials drawn directly from reality, the knowledge or informational function may not only be primary but almost exclusive. Almost exclusive because narrative development, however regulated by informational requirements, nearly always generates an effect which exceeds that of informational transfer or argument alone. In fact, one of the ways in which television criticism has engaged with narrative is precisely in respect of it as a potential distraction device, as a way of engaging the viewer which privileges emotional over rational assessment and which naturalizes aspects of social life which may be the fit subject for questioning and indeed suspicion. Such a negative view of the narrative functions of television has been applied both to fictional and factual output. The kind of criteria which are relevant differ according to genre, notwithstanding the extent to which television's generic system has been recently subject to hybridic mixing (on this, see Chapters 9 and 10).

| General Components of Television Narrative | Many writers on television storytelling have drawn, like literary critics before them, on the categorizations of Vladimir Propp, whose work on Russian fairy tales was first published in 1928 (Fiske 1987 and Kozloff 1992 provide good television-related accounts). Propp discovered patterns of narrative organization which underlay a very wide range of stories. He outlined his account in terms of six phases of narrative development—preparation, complication, transference, struggle, return, and recognition and then further elaborated on the subphases within each. Application of these categories to television may seem to be particularly appropriate given the extent to which popular television fiction trades on cultural tropes and contemporary myth |

in a manner not unlike traditional folk-tale. Silverstone (1981) develops a Proppian analysis of a popular drama series within a broader cultural perspective of this kind. Together with the later work of theorists of narrative form such as Greimas (1966), Todorov (1977), and Barthes (1977), Propp's account has indicated the value of placing the specific, often elaborate, stories of television in the context of the more enduring forms and devices of narrative expression. This is not a quest for a universal theory of narrative (although sometimes a rather ahistorical note is sounded) but an attempt at making deeper connections than might be obtained by a concern framed entirely by the televisual and the contemporary. These connections are formal in the sense that they concern the devices and basic moves by which stories open, develop, progress through various crises and resolutions, and then close. To engage the reader, listener, or viewer, such progressions must create anticipation, even suspense, and delay resolution; they might well repeat certain elements to build up a distinctive thematic/symbolic profile, and they may move around their time-frames (e.g. 'meanwhile', 'many years earlier') to give the story perspective and depth and to allow elaboration on its linear baseline. The connections are also cultural in so far as they indicate generalized linkages between actions or situations and emotions, linkages which can be seen as forms of *affective trope*. Such tropes are those of, say, 'leaving home', 'being isolated among strangers', 'struggling with a superior adversary', 'consolidating friendship'. The tropes have both an individualist dimension (the single acting self), a social one (the self and others), and a broader environmental one (the self in a landscape, the self in the world). To talk thus of a modern television drama is to risk a degree of reductionism in the interests of calling attention to trans-historical and trans-cultural similarities, yet much narrative criticism would want to argue not merely for continuities here at the level of narrative mechanics but at the level of psychological engagement too.

Narrative and Television Studies

I noted earlier that one of the principal concerns of critics and researchers investigating television narrative has been with the implications which narrative form has for viewer knowledge (see Chapter 10). This has been particularly true of a significant strand of work, both in British and American writing on television, which has taken the analysis of ideological forms and consequences as its chief aim (I briefly discussed this strand in my introductory chapter). Writers more concerned with the broader cultural settings of narrative form have also been interested in narrative knowledge but have regarded this in less politically specific terms (instead of ideology, extensive use is made of the ideas of myth and ritual) in order to gain better continuity with pre-modern forms and experiences. For both groups, fictional and non-fictional forms of narrative hold equal interest, the routine popular knowledge of news bulletins exploiting narrative appeal in ways relatable to, if distinct from, the soap opera and the police series. I have already alluded to some of the negative psychological, social, and political consequences often attributed to television narrative form. It might be useful to identify three main lines of critique, often found in combination:

1. Narrative organization in television frequently seduces the viewer into aesthetic relations with what is on screen (e.g. the pleasures of character, of setting, and of action) in a manner which reduces critical distance and inhibits proper engagement with issues. It promotes a form of lazy viewing in contrast to the thoughtful and intensive attention required by many literary, theatrical, and even filmic models (here, the 'critical distancing' practices of Brechtian theatre were a frequent point of positive reference during the debates of the 1970s and 1980s—see particularly MacCabe 1974).

2. Narrative, particularly when applied to non-fictional material, has the effect of oversimplifying what is properly complex and of bringing into a spurious unity what are more properly regarded as diverse elements of an issue. The emphasis upon concrete, visual realizations of story, together with a related avoidance of the abstract, limits expository and interrogatory value. In conventional dramatic practice, narrative often involves high levels of stereotyping in the projection of character (in order to improve recognition and to intensify story values) as well as the use of a number of stock situations and actions as part of the way in which the local details of an account are organized and projected. Here, the connection back to Propp's inventory of folk-tale elements becomes directly relevant. A particular problem is posed by the manner in which many conventional television narratives conclude in a satisfactory resolution of themes. Too often, it is argued, this takes the form of a kind of 'closure', in which thoughts and currents of feeling stimulated by previous depicted action are routed into tidiness and equilibrium by the ending, thus filtering and overmanaging the work of representations upon consciousness.

3. Through the hierarchy of discourses which constitute programmes, whether fictional or non-fictional, certain perspectives on events and circumstances depicted are given an epistemological privileging while others are subordinated, marginalized, or excluded (see category 2 above). Engagement with the story and its characters entails a degree of alignment, however temporary, with dominant viewpoints. However, unlike written fiction, where the narrational voice is often explicit in its judgements on ongoing action, television naturalizes dominant perspectives—they become a function of its modes of portrayal, its camera viewpoints, its scenes of revealed (rather than described) character qualities, all aspects of the realized narrative. By this means, displacements and pseudo-resolutions can be effected without their ideological character being explicit or recognized by the viewer (a character which includes not only what is said and shown but what is *not* being said and shown and what is being implicitly *denied*).

In Britain, although narrative factors were at issue in much pioneer writing about television form (for instance, Williams's idea of 'flow' makes the connection with changing forms of television storytelling—see Chapter 5), it was the journals *Screen* and *Screen Education* which were responsible for developing sustained attention to questions of narrative structure. As so often in television studies, it was the precedent of cinema studies which provided the stimulus here. I remarked above how questions of narrative were frequently interconnected with questions of realism and of ideology, with questions about the power of television to define the world in ways which, whilst appearing obvious, were politically selective. This is particularly so with the debate about 'progressive realism' which took place in these journals. The debate largely followed the terms outlined in an influential article by Colin MacCabe (1974), in which he drew on the ideas of the German dramatist and cultural theorist Bertolt Brecht to develop a critique of the relationship between narrative systems, discursive hierarchies, and the reproduction of dominant ideology. His particular focus was the kind of novelistic mode which installed privileged positions of knowing and worked against active, critical spectatorship (see category 3 above). MacCabe identified these devices of epistemic privileging in the nineteenth-century novel and, despite the radical differences in medium characteristics and dramatic conventions, saw their revised presence in film and in contemporary television drama. Here, it was what was *shown* to the viewer and the manner of its showing which was so unquestioningly installed as the dominant view. A key critical question became: what was wrong about conventional television storytelling and how could it be put right?

One answer came from the critic, Colin McArthur. Citing scenes from a recent drama series *Days of Hope* (BBC 1975), about British working-class history from the First World War to the General Strike of 1926, McArthur (1975) found a fruitful contradiction between what was shown in the visual narrative and the dialogue of some of the characters. This way of undercutting the truth of the spoken accounts of characters from the dominant class by what viewers actually *saw* was a politically progressive approach, argued McArthur, disrupting precisely the narrative orthodoxy against which MacCabe had outlined his 'Brechtian theses'. Yet, in a note of response, MacCabe (1976) disagreed. Using depicted action to indicate the falseness of character speech was, he argued, however progressive the intention, merely to use another method of installing hierarchies within the portrayal and of encouraging viewers to align themselves with a textual 'truth'. It was a different method, certainly, from that of mainstream novelistic naturalism, but its epistemological and political consequences were no less manipulative. MacCabe's argument was for a narrative which was genuinely plural in so far as it confronted the viewer with situations in which difficult interpretative and evaluative choices had to be made, without strategic cueing as to which option was 'correct'.

The debate about progressive realism was, in part, an attempt by television scholars concerned about the politics of drama to redeem realist narrative after a period when a strong anti-realist tendency had asserted its hold on television studies. The difference between MacCabe's and McArthur's positions is indicative of the conflict of opinion on the issue, with MacCabe favouring initiatives at some remove from even the most radical models of television practice and McArthur seeing the potential of current and popular strands of dramatic writing and direction.

In one of the first monographs to pay close and sustained attention to television form, John Ellis (1982) reflected critically on MacCabe's general ideas about narrative models:

> It has been vaguely assumed (though not really practised) that the model of classic film narration could be applied to TV programmes. This is

encouraged by the general assumption of a kind of genealogy of
novelistic narration that Colin MacCabe's version of classic realism at
least is explicitly based upon. MacCabe demonstrates a continuity of
narrational devices from the nineteenth century novel into cinema . . .
this perception is extended by implication to TV, which is seen as taking
cinema's place in its turn. (Ellis 1982: 64)

Ellis notes that the 'material and organizational differences' between the
three media affect the modes of narration available to each, commentating
on the way in which 'the novel's majestic synthesis of its characters and incid-
ents' might be contrasted to 'the fragmentary and often open-ended structure of the TV series' (1982: 66). Developing his own account of television
narration, he puts forward the idea of television as consisting essentially
of 'segments', a consequence of the distinctive conventions of production
within the industry and the representational forms which follow from these
(see my discussion in Chapter 3). Ellis describes segments thus:

> The segment is a relatively self-contained scene which conveys an
> incident, a mood or a particular meaning. Coherence is provided by
> a continuity of character through the segment, or, more occasionally,
> a continuity of place. (Ellis 1982: 148)

He notes a little later that the segment 'does not usually last longer than five
minutes' (1982: 149). The temporal consequences of segmental structure are
also an important factor in his discussion of television 'flow' (see Chapter 6).
Ellis's commentary identifies segmented narrational form as underpinning
both fiction and non-fiction genres, with the differences between the two
realms of far less importance than is usually assumed. Despite this, it is evident in his chapter on television narration that it is the popular drama series
which provides the focus:

> The characteristic form of series narration is that of the continuous
> update, returning to the present and leaving a question or a cliff-hanger
> for the future. Overall, it is a form of narration that lends itself to the
> exploration of incidents and their repercussions in terms of inter-
> personal psychology. It habitually deals with a larger number of
> characters than the cinematic narration, and can concern itself more
> with their interaction and nuances of behaviour. It is an extensive form
> rather than a consecutive one. Similar narrational forms can be found at
> the levels of fiction and of non-fiction. There is no real difference in
> narrational form between news and soap opera. The distinction is at
> another level: that of the source of the material. (Ellis 1982: 158–9)

Even allowing a certain liberty of generalization in the interests of provocative commentary (Ellis shows himself well aware of this kind of play-off) it
is hard to agree with the final comment. The characteristic form of in-studio
direct address from the news desk, interspersed by a series of location reports
containing commentary over film and interviews, seems to involve a very
different mode of narrative organization from the *mise-en-scène*, characterization, dialogue, and musical cueing of popular serial drama. There is a distinction in the 'source of the material' it is true, but there is also a profound
distinction in the management of looks and sounds to engage the viewer in

the business of story-following and the generation of story values. The way in which the imagination works upon what is presented upon the screen in the two instances raises quite separate questions of perception and understanding. Useful generalizations can be made about television narrative (Ellis has been justly influential here), but the differentiations of television's generic system also warrant attention too.

Whatever the suggestiveness of the segment idea for the exploration of television narrative at the time Ellis was writing in the early 1980s it is, as I noted in Chapter 3, now inappropriate to the range of narrative visualizations which current television, with its changed technology and methods of production, displays. A much more dynamic and mobile range of options for storytelling is now being employed in everything from news, advertisements, and documentaries to single dramas and soaps. This new hyperactivity is starting to modify the terms of narrative critique. Distinguishing between narratives whose shifts and interruptions are, indeed, part of a more provocative, participatory invitation to an assumed intelligent audience and those in which they are essentially fashionable, stylistic markers, has become an issue in recent criticism (see, for instance, the essays in Lusted and Geraghty 1997).

Narrative and Genre: Three Foci

I want now to move down from the level of general commentary and look at three areas which have attracted particular attention from analysts of television narrative. These are news, documentary, and soaps—each presenting a different formal profile and a different set of questions about pleasure and knowledge too.

■ News

The narrative dimension of news is recognized within the profession of journalism itself by the use of the term 'story' to describe what it is that journalists work on. Not surprisingly, however, 'stories' are usually regarded as the *pre*-journalistic happenings themselves, the referents of reporting, rather than the product of journalistic discourse, although much journalistic training concerns itself with ways of fashioning accounts not only for clarity but for continuity and impact. There is, then, a self-conscious aesthetics of journalism, of which a good part concerns narrative organization.

However, television news storytelling relies heavily on *spoken* rather than *enacted* narrative (to use the distinction I outlined above). No matter how strong its pictorial support (such as might be available, for instance, in location reporting from a scene where filmable and newsworthy action is occurring) a good deal of telling has to accompany the showing. The continuity and narrative coherence of the images themselves (together with actuality speech and sound) are, in most reports, of a low order. Spatial and temporal shifts, considerable restriction in scopic mobility (e.g. the inability to pursue unfolding action in detail and from shifting perspectives), and the brevity of the conventional report, do not allow for a number of options which every director of fictional narrative would expect to have available. Added to this, there is the fact that, even in the most 'infotainment'-style formats, the work of exposition has to be done within the news story. Journalistic discourses of exposition variously entail the citing of statistics, the advancing of rival versions of causality, the close description of physical conditions, speculation on probable consequences, the accessing of witnesses and experts, etc. Such expository work gives much journalistic storytelling an informational loading which frequently resists continuous narrative shaping. The story is interrupted and/or slowed down in a manner which fiction, even of the most experimental kind, would find a severe limitation on its appeal (I have discussed the exposition/narrative tensions of television news at greater length in Corner 1995). A further, related point here concerns how news stories end. However much journalists attempt to tie things together (often with a piece-to-camera before handing back to the studio), narrative resolution in journalism has, for the most part, neither the aesthetic scope nor the referential licence to bring its stories to a conclusion in the manner of fiction.

One of the few ways in which journalists can attempt to provide a more continuous and deeper narrative structure for their stories is by recourse to dramatization, either in whole or in part. When scenes are enacted for the camera, then a whole range of formal possibilities (e.g. close-ups, cutaways, parallel action, expressive angles, compositions and lighting, music to cue mood) can be introduced. Not surprisingly, there are professional codes of restraint on the use of this approach, quite apart from the difficulty of applying it to many routine news items. In their pioneering study of newsroom methods, Ericson, Baranek, and Chan (1987) looked at different levels at which narrative support was provided by staged visuals, including a case of extensive dramatization (a drug seizure story) all the more controversial since, mixed with actuality material, the dramatized reconstruction was not identified on screen for what it was. Yet even here, continuity was only maintained by the voice-over speech of the reporter providing a steady flow of information, a discursive usage quite alien to most contemporary forms of fiction.

With strong originality, Justin Lewis (1985) tackles the question of news narrative from the perspective of viewer comprehension and memory. In fact, Lewis is original not only in the framing of his research but also because he sees the news as under-narrativized, in sharp contrast to many researchers who, as I have suggested, variously regard the current manifestations of narrative journalism as subverting expositional integrity. Lewis takes the novel step of rewriting a news item which his research has shown to have posed difficulties of understanding for viewers.

This story is about a politician addressing a public meeting during a sensitive point in his career when the response of his audience will be significant. Lewis criticizes the original for two main faults. First of all, the introduction to the item gives the story's ending away thus losing the lure of what will happen next from the report itself. Secondly, voice-over and visuals are not matched tightly enough, dispersing viewer understanding across the two elements and creating the possibility for interpretative mistakes. Lewis's rewrite has an introduction which does not indicate how things end and a main report which holds more firmly to chronology and keeps spoken narration tight to pictures. It is also more explicit about the political context for understanding the item rather than relying on prior viewer knowledge. To many viewers, his revised version might well seem condescending both in the basic nature of the offered background and its use of a teaser element in the unfolding of the report. Even his tighter sound/picture matching carries a degree of didactic directness missing from the original, which offers a looser, colloquial account across its images. Lewis's examination of the play-off between narrativization and understanding is, however, a valuable piece of television research and his approach could usefully be incorporated into future studies as news, internationally, undergoes a major restyling (on this, see for instance Dahlgren 1995).

■ **Documentary**   The question of narrative in documentary is similar in many respects to that in news. Documentary is frequently a vehicle for exposition. This exposition is mostly grounded in to-camera and voice-over speech, and the combination of presenter speech and images is often interspersed with the accessed voices of interviewees. Since many documentaries are concerned with the character and causality of other than physical events, their visualizations, like news, regularly need the support of speech, whether offered directly by a presenter or indirectly by those portrayed. Yet documentary is a more expansive form of representation than news, able to develop values of duration, to stay with unfolding action for several minutes, and to carry out an intensive filming of its topic followed by considered and lengthy phases of editing. Documentary film and television has two broad formats in which the narrative dimension is especially prominent. In the drama-documentary, re-enactment of events allows the introduction of narrative shaping and the realization of local action in a manner comparable with fiction. In the observational 'fly-on-the-wall' mode, sustained observation of an unfolding circumstance or act provides strong chronological and durational values. The plane of the observed comes to have close parallels with a fictive diegesis, the plane of an observed fictional narrative, albeit with far less scope for directorial management (although editing allows for the substantial *post-facto* shaping of what might appear to be direct relay).

Between these two poles of full theatricality and observationalism, however, documentary has a whole range of options for narrativizing its materials, both across the film or programme as a whole and locally, within the terms of a specific scene. For instance, particular episodes in a documentary otherwise structured in terms of expositional development can develop strong narrative values by the temporary use of dramatization using actors, or by strongly proactive shooting methods (for example, a woman's journey home from work, filmed with strong direction of *the mise-en-scène*, actions, and facial expressions and with perhaps several takes to achieve good levels of continuity and scopic interest).

So documentary is narrativized in different ways and to different 'thicknesses'. Can it ever be without narrative? Two of the major studies in documentary form, Nichols (1991) and Winston (1995) suggest not, although they acknowledge the very wide range of narrative systems and methods. Winston, in an excellent discussion of narrative and chronology, takes issue with the film theorists Bordwell and Thompson (1990) for including documentary in their chapter on 'nonnarrative formal systems'. Even the most expository, descriptive, thematically organized documentaries, argues Winston, have a certain irreducible level of narrative structuring. This question of narrative levels, in relation to which I have used the impressionistic terms 'thick' and 'thin', is an important one for many debates. In a way which is relevant for the arguments developed earlier in this chapter, Nichols and Winston also completely reject the idea that the presence of narrative is by itself an indicator of fictionality. Narrative is, they argue, an aspect of many different kinds of discourse including scientific and historical ones. Thus they reject the position which seeks to undercut documentary status simply by pointing to narrative functions.

Since documentary has such a wide range of narrative options, and a long history of variously employing them, it is not surprising that it also has a rich theoretical literature on the topic. On the whole, this has been more thoughtful and productive than that on storytelling in news. Given that documentaries do have a level of narrative organization (variously repressed or projected), the literature has asked: how does narrative work in *this* film or programme and with what aesthetic and cognitive consequences for the viewer?

With the new emphasis on spectacle in many genres of television, there has been an intensification of action-oriented narrative values in documentary programmes (particularly in series). This has been seen by some critics to detract from the level of argument and explanation (see Chapter 10). Such work delivers, it is claimed, not 'the shock of understanding' but the pleasure of setting and the diversion and the thrill of action. Recently, criticism of this kind has been made of 'reality tv' formats (see Nichols 1994 and Bondebjerg 1996), which have used both dramatization and observational modes of narrative to new levels of intensity and with an eclectic stylization which is at risk of making any referential function quite secondary to the attractions of the representation itself.

■ **Series, serials, and soaps**

Soaps may be seen as a special case of television narrative organization, a form (more correctly, a range of forms) which has drawn much critical interest.

A distinction between *series* and *serial* forms is useful in exploring current formats and developments and in placing soaps within their broader context of extended television storytelling. With *series* forms a number of narrative characteristics not found in feature film fiction appear. In the television series, although the end of each episode conventionally concludes a main plot, cross-programme continuity is achieved by an increasing familiarity with the main characters, with the setting, and with background story-lines which may run throughout the entire series. A lot of work which a feature film has to do in order to establish characters and setting is not necessary after the initial episode and the development of story-lines can be achieved more economically with such a degree of already established detail. Of course, overreliance on prior knowledge would quickly lead to individual episodes becoming incomprehensible when viewed independently, and so a degree of concise repetition is often built into the opening minutes of each programme.

Given the level of routine, industrial production involved in making a television series and the economics associated with this, relative confinement to studio settings and limited editing options were a feature of low-to-middle-budget projects for many years, as Ellis comments (see my discussion of his general account of television narrative above). This gave many series narratives a rather interior, static quality when compared to those of film. However, new technology has pulled series drama ever further away from its origins in studio productions recorded in a single run-through or transmitted live (see Briggs 1995: 832–9). Series have become flexible in their employment of single episode and multi-episode plot strands and, following American precedents, they have often developed complex, multistrand narratives, switching to and from concurrent lines of action during the course of an episode. This is most notable in workplace-based series, those featuring hospitals and police stations in particular, where both the size of the cast and the nature of the occupation allow for such diversity.

The possibilities offered by having an established fictional world already known to the viewer are increased in *serial* drama. Some short-run serials (e.g. four to twelve episodes) are essentially dramas with a single main storyline around which more elaboration of subplot and, especially, of character is permissible than in the single play or film. The scheduling opportunities which this form offers and its cultural reach (in terms, for instance, of book tie-ins) has been extensively exploited in recent British television. However, it is the long-running serials which are able to develop the most distinctive (and for any study of television's social impact, most significant) narrative features. Here, there is strong continuity across episodes and usually a very high level of continuity in the cast. Whereas the imaginative centre of many series dramas is a kind of work (e.g. hospital doctor, policeman, private detective), the imaginative centre of many serials is place and people. As many critics have noted, community at the level of the family unit and then the neighbourhood is perhaps the key ingredient in the television soap opera (a point developed in Geraghty 1991).

The soap typically presents long-term deep-level plots about relationships, upon which various middle- and short-term story-lines are developed. Whereas it might be possible to describe a feature film plot in terms of a single, dynamically developing narrative line, a soap is a slow-moving, multi-decker project, heavy with character depth and biography, and with the implications which actions, words, and looks carry, often to be teased out in subsequent episodes. Devices of focalization (see Branigan 1992), by which the perspectives of specific characters temporarily guide our narrative understanding, can be variously used in complementary or antagonistic ways. Repetition is a necessary part of the narrative rhythm of soap, a factor in its production of familiarity with the fictive world of a specific (usually domestic) grouping, working through experiences and relationships over time. Against this pattern of steady predictability, change and disruption in the soap can be used with considerable force (innovative mixes for combining continuity with change are, in the mid-1990s, both a feature of new soaps and the revamping of older ones).

Perhaps the most important feature of soap narrative is durational. As Christine Geraghty says (1991: 11), 'time rather than action' is its basis.

Viewers typically experience episodes of their favourite soap opera as a routine engagement with an imagined world running concurrently with their own real one. The frequency of episode transmission (on current British television, often either daily or two or three times a week) reinforces this kind of viewing relationship. Soap narratives also follow a calendar coextensive with that followed by audiences, although there is considerable variation in the way soaps choose to register and comment upon the ongoing public world.

The lack of final closure in soap narrative, the depth of the virtual relationship which viewers enjoy with characters (either positively or negatively), and the sense of coexistence between real and fictive worlds which frames the viewing experience, all produce a distinctive socio-aesthetic profile. Around successful series, there develops a dense culture of gossip, exploiting the possibilities of star/role ambiguity. Soaps are, internationally, the most popular televisual form and their narrative modes are a significant factor in modern storytelling (the essays in Allen 1995 document both these aspects well).

The narrative practices of television, incorporating both speech and enactment and frequently addressed to the viewer within domestic space and within the time-frames of the routine and the everyday, are a principal feature of modern popular culture. Their presence in journalism, documentary, and current affairs output as well as in drama means that they are also a significant dimension of modern public knowledge. Although sometimes regarded as a self-evident indicator of trivialization or of distortion when found outside of fiction, narrative organization is a necessary underlying principle of many broadcast forms. However, this should not lead us to ignore its changing varieties, the importance of plotting their implications and, where necessary, of questioning the integrity of their use. A lack of adequate differentiation between narrative types has, I think, been a deficiency in much criticism and research. The forms of television narrative are undergoing change in kind and in application, making precision in analysis of their ways of generating knowledge and pleasure more necessary than ever.

6
Flow

'**FLOW**' is a word which occurs regularly in studies of television, with many uses referring back to Raymond Williams's 1974 discussion in *Television: Technology and Cultural Form*. Of course, the idea of flow may seem quite an apt metaphor for the general process of television—a steady outpouring of images and sounds from channels and stations into homes and (with transformations *en route*) the minds of viewers, often with a high level of continuity across the various genres and formats. Like theatre and film, television is a temporal medium, using producer-controlled duration as part of its aesthetics. Unlike them, but like radio, its performances do not occur as sharply discrete events, contextualized by social action (e.g. going to the theatre or the cinema) but are located within the system of a channel schedule. The schedule organizes a series of programmes, all of which are on television on a given night. The titles and character of these programmes will not be known by a number of viewers until the items are announced on-air or their title sequences begin. In this context, an 'evening's viewing' may often provide a more agreeable way of watching television than the selection of one specific programme. Some uses of 'flow' simply pick up on the term in this common-sense way and do not wish to give it any more ambitious, conceptual meaning.

Williams begins from this level of meaning. However, the way in which he developed and employed the notion, and then the debate about this—a debate including criticism and attempted revision—has given flow almost a semi-technical meaning in many studies and has provided a point of reference for argument about a number of important formal and thematic features of the medium. Flow has become a notion of self-evident critique, carrying with it negative assumptions about television's temporality and power and the viewing relationships which it encourages. It will be the general judgement of this chapter that the term cannot really sustain the weight of theory which has often been placed upon it, and indeed that in some commentaries it might be viewed as a diversion from proper conceptual development. Flow has become something of a totem in television theory internationally. In a book of this kind, a trip through some of the disagreements which it has generated is useful. More than in other chapters, then, I shall be involved here in the pursuit of an intellectual history.

Williams on Flow   In Williams (1974) the idea makes its appearance in chapter 4, 'Programming: distribution and flow', where, in the introduction, it is noted that it is 'necessary to go beyond the static concept of "distribution" to the mobile concept of "flow" ' (Williams 1974: 78). In the early part of this chapter (section A), Williams outlines the 'distributive' character of television by reference to the different programme categories found in a week's sampling of British television in Spring 1973. The distribution is presented in tabular form, including indications of comparative percentages. Section B is subtitled 'Programming as sequence or flow' and contains the core of Williams's ideas about the phenomenon and his analytic perspective upon it. The 'characteristic organisation' of developed broadcasting systems and 'therefore the characteristic experience' is one of 'sequence or flow' he comments, 'planned flow is then perhaps the defining characteristic of broadcasting' (Williams 1974: 86). There then follows this passage, noting that the significance of the difference between broadcasting and previous cultural forms lies not merely in the distribution to the home, but:

> It is that the real programme that is offered is a *sequence* or set of alternative sequences of these and other similar events [Williams has referred earlier to plays, meetings, and stories] which are then available in a single dimension and in a single operation. (Williams 1974: 87, italics in original)

Two pages later, Williams remarks how there has been a move from 'programming' to 'flow' in television which has been hard to identify in Britain because of the continued presence of the earlier notion in industrial practice:

> There has been a significant shift from the concept of sequence as *programming* to the concept of sequence as *flow*. Yet this is difficult to see because the older concept of programming—the temporal sequence within which mix and proportion and balance operate—is still active and still to some extent real. (Williams 1974: 89, italics in original)

The emphasis here is on the residual element of public service broadcasting (mix, proportion, and balance) in contexts where new industrial imperatives are changing the terms of programme sequencing. Williams notes that it has been through his work as a television reviewer (for the weekly magazine, the *Listener*) that he has become aware of flow as a factor in his own viewing experience. The inter-programme perspective continues over the next page or so of his account, with the arrival of interruptions to programme sequence in the form of commercials (in Britain, from 1955) being seen as a decisive moment in the development of flow, a moment so significant that, in fact, it quite quickly made the very idea of interruption inadequate to describe the change:

> What is being offered is not, in older terms, a programme of discrete units with particular insertions, but a planned flow, in which the true series is not the published sequence of programme items but this sequence transformed by the inclusion of another kind of sequence, so that these sequences together compose the real flow. (Williams 1974: 90)

The increasing use of trailers for forthcoming programmes, inserted within the programme sequence, is also cited as a further example of the new temporal regime, making it true of non-commercial as well as of commercial channels. It is the kind of macro-flow created by a mixture of programmes, commercials, and trailers which Williams describes in his much-cited account of a personal, and traumatic, early encounter with flow. This occurred, not surprisingly, on a trip to America and is worth citing at some length:

> One night in Miami, still dazed from a week on an Atlantic liner, I began watching a film and at first had some difficulty in adjusting to a much greater frequency of commercial 'breaks'. Yet this was a minor problem compared to what eventually happened. Two other films, which were to be shown on the same channel on other nights, began to be inserted as trailers. A crime in San Francisco (the subject of the original film) began to operate in an extraordinary counterpoint not only with the deodorant and cereal commercials but with a romance in Paris and the eruption of a prehistoric monster who laid waste New York.

He goes on to note that, unlike in Britain, there was here no sign of an interval, 'the transitions from film to commercial and from film A to films B and C were in effect unmarked'. Summing up this experience, he comments:

> I can still not be sure what I took from that whole flow. I believe I registered some incidents as happening in the wrong film, and some characters in the commercials as involved in the film episodes, in what came to seem—for all the occasional bizarre disparities—a single irresponsible flow of images and feelings. (Williams 1974: 91–2)

It is worth pointing out straight away that, of course, Williams is here reporting the experience of a cultural outsider, still disoriented through travel and fresh to American television. His personal encounter offers a way into analysis but it does not document the televisual experience of the American viewer precisely because of its lack of familiarity with the new conventions. Williams is explicitly reporting from outside the culture but the relation between inside and outside, and then more particularly the relationship between television sequence and viewer experience, are important factors in the debate about flow.

We can also note from the last quotation that flow is essentially experienced as a kind of entity holding together local disparities, it presents a mode of higher unity. Moreover, it is seen as constituted both out of representations themselves and the forms of subjective affect ('images *and* feelings') and is 'irresponsible'. Although Williams is keen to keep an analytic focus rather than to elaborate judgements, it is clear that throughout his account flow is part of a pathology of television, a bad feature of general programme organization rooted in commercial conditions of production.

It is at this point that attention is moved down again to the level of intra-programme relationships. Williams notes how programmes are internally divided to meet the demands of the commercial breaks and how 'strong openings' are required to keep viewers watching, often very quickly followed by a 'break' (the significance of multi-channel competition for the aesthetics of flow, later to be extensively discussed by other researchers, here begins to appear in the argument). He remarks how 'the interest aroused must be strong enough to initiate the expectation of (interrupted but sustainable) sequence' and, linking inter-programme with intra-programme organization, goes on to observe: 'Thus a quality of the external sequence becomes a mode of definition of an internal method' (Williams 1974: 92). He reflects on the general implications of the previous pages, which mix together conceptual debate, recounted experience, and analysis. What, then, is 'flow'?

> . . . the replacement of a programme series of timed, sequential units by a flow series of differently related units in which the timing, though real, is undeclared, and in which the real internal organisation is something other than the declared organisation. (Williams 1974: 93)

Flow is not only a meta-process then, it is also a clandestine one.

In formulations which sometimes lack a final clarity, it is in these pages of *Television* that Williams puts the emphasis on a new kind of programme sequence which has so radically broken with the older idea of a string of discrete items, even one with interruptions, as to constitute a fresh mode altogether. This mode, initially a matter of inter-programme order, has had implications for intra-programme relations too, changing the rhythm, pace, and general aesthetic economy of generic formats and encouraging short, intensive sequences as the principal units of programme building. This new, interpenetrating mixture of sights and sounds is experienced by the viewer as having a kind of meta-coherence despite a lack of logical, thematic relations between parts. Such experiencing is at least partly the product of a covert process, in which a 'declared' form of organization is in fact displaced by another. This is judged to be culturally bad (although we may note that it is not the same thing at all as that self-conscious confusion which Williams recounts after his Miami viewing). One further point is perhaps worth remarking on here—Williams comments on how flow is now organized precisely to discourage switching off. The strengthening of the 'impulse to go on watching' (1974: 94) is clearly seen to be a factor in the badness of flow.

Having laid out his general ideas in this way, introducing in the process some uncertainties of emphasis, Williams moves to several pages of detailed analysis. At this point, a firmer typology is introduced (1974: 96). Examples of flow are to be examined in relation to 'three different orders of detail'. First, there is the flow within an evening's programmes. Williams indicates this by simply listing the start times of the various items on selected channels. Secondly, there is what he calls 'the more evident flow of the actual succession of items within and between the published sequence of units'. This is a level at which 'relative unification' of the 'diverse' is apparent. Williams indicates this level by taking in turn an American and a British evening news programme and blocking out the movement, down the programme, of studio-presented and filmed-report items. We shift here to a focus on intraprogramme relations. Finally, there is 'the really detailed flow within this general movement', the 'actual succession of words and images'. Here, Williams takes two or three items from the American news magazine previously outlined in his second level analysis and opens out a full transcription with indication of visuals.

What are the findings of this three-level analysis? At the first stage, Williams notes the factors of schedule-building, including 'shift points' and phases of relative homogeneity. In assessing the two evening news magazines at the second level, he notes the 'fusion' across miscellany and the 'exclusion of certain kinds of connection and contrast'. Although he does not use the term, it is the 'packaging' of items into a viewable whole, according to a scheme of newsroom priorities, which attracts his charge of 'undiscriminating'. He notes how the British programme relies less on personality appeal than the American one, but how it still works to manage, shift, and sustain 'emotional tone' by devices of continuity which follow a given 'structure of feeling' (1974: 111). It is the third level which produces the most detailed and ambitious commentary. In the detail of the American news items, Williams notes a 'hurried blur' (1974: 116), nothing is 'fully reported', 'pace and style' are everything. This he finds to be in contrast with the 'cool deliberation' of the commercials, where repetition is also strategically used. Certain recurring values and themes in the news set up an *internal* pattern within the television discourse despite the highly diverse external references which items carry.

As a way of extending and substantiating the earlier, general argument about flow, it seems to me that these analyses are rather disappointing, and this is perhaps one of the reasons why they are cited and discussed less than one might expect given the attention that the notion itself has received. The first level's framing in terms of listed schedules and then the second and third level's shift to internal programme organization, albeit with commercial inserts, fits a little oddly with the earlier emphasis on the articulation across programmes, the experience within schedule. The news programmes analysed are read in a way which is essentially schedule independent, their own discreteness is confirmed by the critical attention they receive. Secondly, there is something unsatisfactory about news taking up so much of the analysis. The exercise effectively turns into a commentary about the changing terms of broadcast journalism, interspersed with critical remarks about the culturally exploitative character of television advertising. Despite the institutional centrality of news services to broadcast television, how important is the experience of news to the general experience of flow? The increasingly slicker treatment of numerous and diverse items gives the news a flow profile of a very distinctive kind—how does its analysis relate to the larger phenomenon? It seems as if Williams's selection here is guided by concerns other than the flow thesis, that his focus on news follows a more specific interest in the changing modes of public information. Whatever the importance of these, they cannot on their own exemplify just how 'the flow of meanings and values of a specific culture' (1974: 118) is managed by television. The new structuring of cultural perception which is indicated in the general discussion does not really get either documented or developed in these analytic pages.

The Debate about Flow

Cited approvingly within the academic television criticism of the late 1970s, though not with much interest in either development or application, flow became established as a term of the emerging television studies. One of the first writers to take explicit issue with it was John Ellis, in his influential study *Visible Fictions*, published in 1982. His general judgement is that, despite its suggestiveness, '[t]he notion of flow is a much misused one, and its openness to misuse is the result of the way in which Williams defines the idea' (1982: 117). Ellis's own recurrent concern in his chapters on television is with the 'segmental' nature of television in its early 1980s form, that is, its extensive use of standard-length, programme building blocks consisting of several shots but sustaining a focus on the same action and setting (see my discussion in Chapters 3 and 5). Segmentalism, for Ellis, is both a function of television's typical mode of studio production and cost efficiency and a requirement of the medium's need to hold the viewer with a particular mixture of change and continuity. Ellis finds segmental organization not only in news (where it is, as I noted above, almost there by definition) and commercials (where the durational values permit of little else) but also in popular drama. Ellis sees his idea as owing some debt to Williams's flow and to the notion of a shift in the nature of the 'timed sequential units' out of which television is constituted. Noting that there is a degree of imprecision and perhaps of uncertainty in Williams's formulations, Ellis goes on to comment that 'Williams's underestimates the complexity of broadcast TV's commodity form, which has very little to do with the single text' (1982: 118). He sees Williams as working with a model of the 'cinema-style text' (1982: 118) which is then compromised by flow. It is true that Williams's demonstration of textuality within flow is limited by his selection of news programmes, but news is clearly *not* a cinema-style text and just what degree of inviolability he is working with as an ideal for different genres is never fully clear.

Rick Altman, in a valuable essay (1986) on the importance of sound in television (largely taking its cue from Ellis's book), incorporates flow into his own account of how television works. However, he first of all wants to correct what he sees as a tendency for Williams to regard flow as simply a function of 'the television experience itself' rather than of a particular kind of commercial television system (1986: 40). In fact, although Williams occasionally suggests generalization to the medium *per se*, it is pretty clear from his other comments that the specificity of commercial scheduling in a ratings system is well understood by him to be an important factor in flow development. Altman wants to connect television flow to another form of flow, 'household flow'—the routines and times of everyday living—and to argue a greater complexity in the way that inter-channel competition produces flow structures. Flow occurs when channels, in response to competition, develop a (sound-led) strategy of appeal which aims to increase the amount of time when the set is switched on even if not watched in households and thus to improve ratings by a kind of fraud (1986: 44). But there are exceptions. Some channels (for instance, those carrying feature films only) may not respond to competition in this way, so they have to use other means of building and holding audiences. Altman's point about scheduling strategies is well made, but his own version of flow does not directly connect with the kind of representational, perceptual, and cognitive matters with which Williams is grappling. Moreover, 'household flow' begins to stretch the notion a little beyond the point of usefulness—that households have routines and schedules internalized by their members we can readily agree (see Chapter 8 on this), but calling it flow in a way which supposedly matches Williams's usage merely underlines the problems of precision which the term courts.

One year later, in his synoptic and widely used textbook *Television Culture* (1987) John Fiske takes up the issue of flow within the terms of his own emphasis on the multiple meaning potential of television's texts ('polysemy') and on variable viewer interpretation. He finds it a term too unsympathetic to the cultural character of television. Williams's criticism of flow 'seems to derive from his literary desire for a named author to be responsible for a text, and for this responsibility to be exercised in the production of a coherent, unified text' (1987: 100). In fact, this wish for named authorship, a charge to some extent following Ellis's earlier line of critique, is very hard to find in Williams's account, even as an implication. Coherence becomes an issue specifically to do with the logical relations, or lack of them, within the news sequences analysed. Fiske, in reference to Williams, questions the idea that television flow is 'random or unstructured' but Williams certainly does *not* think this, since he describes it as 'planned' and sees one of its effects as precisely the giving of a sense of continuity and shape (culturally specific and industrially strategic) to what is watched. Fiske considers Williams's more substantive analyses but he describes the scheme as providing 'two levels of analysis' (1987: 100) when in fact there are three. In assessing what Williams has to say here, he misses out the close attention to word and image sequence in the news (at level three, 'close-range analysis') which is arguably the most engaging part of the chapter. In considering the level two analysis of American news ('medium-range analysis'), Fiske takes issue with the way in which lack of explicit connection becomes a problem for Williams:

> What he does not see is that the lack of connections opens the text up—the relationship between the Wounded Knee item and the promo for the Western, for instance, can be read from a progressive or a reactionary position. (Fiske 1987: 101)

Fiske wants to read the only partially closed character of flow as an invitation to active viewing and not a breach of some principle of intra- and intertextual integrity. Significantly, Fiske also cites Ellis (1982) on segmentalism (see above), in support of the idea that 'the disruptive breaks between segments outweigh any attempts of continuity or consequence to unify the text' (1987: 103). Now this idea really does raise some problems for the notion of flow. For if 'breaks' rather than 'continuity' characterize the television experience, one very strong element of the whole flow notion—that viewers are somehow or other caught up in a meta-perceptual frame (a kind of world-view) which works above disparity and variety—has to be abandoned.

I shall return to these difficult questions concerning the supposed cognitive and affective profile of flow at the end of this chapter, but there are two points which it may be useful to remark on here, however self-evident they may be. First of all, the unitariness of flow for Williams appears to be a matter of a general, television-induced pattern of continuities in tone, themes, value, and effect ('structures of feeling') in the material, it is not some determinate total meaning. In his disoriented Miami experience, of course, attending to the culture as a non-member, it is confusion rather than totalization which comes through most strongly. Whatever the context, to talk of the total meaning of flow is immediately to push an already awkward notion straight up into metaphysics. Secondly, it seems clear that whatever the erosion of firm generic boundaries in programming and the forward momentum of the schedule, a significant part of the audience for a significant amount of time is likely to be differentiating between the separate items on the channel(s) they are watching. Moreover, they will be differentiating in a way which informs switching on, channel changing, and switching off. Indeed, some of the newer forms of 'quality' television described illuminatingly in Caldwell (1995) make a great effort to establish the firmest textual borders they can. As Caldwell puts it, 'the bounds of distinction are in fact a crucial part of the genre' (1995: 163). It sometimes seems that discussion of flow gets caught between equally impossible poles. On the one hand, there is mass, undifferentiated depiction. Jane Feuer's comments about a 'continuous, never-ending sequence in which it is *impossible* to separate out individual texts' (italics added) stands as a good indication of inflationary claims-making here (Feuer 1983: 15). On the other hand, anarchic levels of disruption and discontinuity are seen to flourish. Just why so many programmes on so many channels appear to have hung on to a fair degree of stable generic identity in the context of such dissolving pressures is a question which might have been asked more often. As Jostein Gripsrud notes in a shrewd, recent commentary (1997), individual programme identity is a clear feature of current audience uses of television not merely something ascertainable by textual analysis.

I have indicated above that deciding how to work with the idea of flow has caused problems for many researchers, often turning initial appreciation of Williams's insightfulness into complaints about his lack of precision. In particular, the play-off between the more objective dimension of flow, as a matter of textual organization, and its more subjective dimension, as a matter of viewing experience, has proved troublesome. Fiske's critical location of the term within his own brand of liberatory semiotics takes one route out of this, whereas Ellis's focus directs our attention more towards the ways in which television is produced.

A stimulating discussion of the problems which the term has caused is offered in Dienst (1994). Dienst is alert to the way in which 'a theoretical merging of transmission and reception' is attempted by the term and to the variety of ways in which flow has been seen as a macro-experience of coherence or of confusion or, indeed, somehow of both at the same time! Dienst also comments on the importance of sound to the construction of flow effects, citing the valuable contribution made by Altman (1986), discussed above, to the analysis of television sound and its consequences. In attempting to tease out the different directions in which speculation about flow has gone, he formulates the widespread feeling that television works against memory:

> television survives through flow, whose transmission washes away the particularity of its messages along with the differences between them, and whose reception drains perception of its resistant holding powers of distance and memory. (Dienst 1994: 33)

However, as I have already noted, any judgements as to the loss of particularity and drained memory would have to pay much closer attention to the specific ways in which television output is attended to, talked about, and used in contemporary culture.

The most substantive attempt to rethink flow in relation to the new (in some countries, only slowly emerging) conditions of multi-channel availability is that undertaken by Klaus Bruhn Jensen (1995). Jensen moves both outwards, to register the range of channel options within which viewing now frequently occurs, and also inwards, to examine the kinds of customized flow which results from individual viewer choices. His analysis, carried out with respondent viewers who had their viewing shifts recorded through a VCR hook-up, provides an objective mapping of two lines of flow—the sequences issuing from available channels and then the movements and durational values across and within these sequences constituted by the viewer's channel changes and viewing periods. A third level of analysis allows a plotting of the total of *possible* sequences in terms of a 'superflow'. Heterogeneous though this most broad of flows might seem to be, constructed as it is from the different and often coextensive flow options, Jensen explores the extent to which its cultural 'superthemes', the general categories within which its contents fall, are in fact quite limited in range. The main argument to emerge from Jensen's project is that the exercising of increased channel choice does not necessarily remove viewers from the downward cultural constraints of flow, it merely places their viewing within a different, more expansive, flow context. In fact, although he starts with the debate about flow as it has developed out of Williams's work, Jensen's primary concern is neither with depictive organization nor with viewing experience as such, but with television's cultural thematics. Thus the notion slips back into what I earlier called its more common-sense meaning, despite the originality and value of Jensen's work taken on its own terms.

The Limitations of an Idea

In tracing some of the history of the debate about flow, a number of problems of clarity of definition and discontinuity of emphasis have been noted. One broader, overarching problem is worth remarking on, although it has been implicitly indicated earlier. It is the problem of essentialism, whereby use of the idea of flow, wittingly or not, produces in the analysis an essential television artefact along with its related experience. It is a tendency consonant with a totalizing imperative in certain strands of television criticism: television has always to be seen in sum; attention to the parts is never enough. We can see this coming through in Stephen Heath's synoptic and wide-ranging article 'Representing Television' (1990). Here he is talking of the need for research and analysis to counter the steady naturalization of television which is occurring through other institutions in society:

> There is a necessary struggle for meaning but [it] cannot proceed as though it were just a question of more texts to be read, deconstructed, revealed in their radical contradictions; the unity of the program after all is precisely a unity—a term—of television, which latter needs to be as much (and more) in the analysis as it is in the program. (Heath 1990: 296)

The unity here looks very much like one which is theoretically imposed and, what is more, licensing itself to be so. The totalization goes along with a pessimism—television as the 'bad machine'—which outdoes that of Williams:

> the task is to make the critical distance that television continually erodes in its extension, its availability, its proximity—all of which is played out on its screen from show to show in the endless flow. (Heath 1990: 297)

Later, such pessimism is further underlined and gains a grander magnitude, 'the perpetual flow of a constant present without any hope beyond its repetition' (1990: 297).

This kind of philosophical despairing of television is, it seems to me, in a logical relationship with Williams's own ideas sixteen years earlier. Its level of generality, the very terms of its formulation, are such as to prevent it acting to inform substantive criticism and research.

The concept of flow has nearly always carried tones of regret at anonymous, mass cultural production (in this respect, Fiske is right to remark on the significance of the literary critical dimensions of Williams's work). It has opened up a debate about the ways in which television's cultural profile and terms of cultural performance are distinctive, but as Gripsrud brings out very well (1997), it has generally done little to help specific analysis of formal structures because it has been pulled relentlessly towards the macro and the speculative. It is also suggestive about the new conditions of television viewing as an experience of dense intertextuality occurring within specific (and changing) kinds of temporal context. Yet the confusion about whether flow is primarily disorientation or some kind of politically suspect meta-meaning (an issue essentially about the semantics of flow) is only one of the problems which have proved an obstacle to development here. Moreover, productive exploration of the different kinds of television time has been pursued by writers outside of the debate about flow, most suggestively by Paddy Scannell (1996), drawing on work in phenomenology as well as a detailed engagement with broadcasting history. Assumptions about the power of the 'flow effect', deriving from metaphoric suggestiveness, have also been treacherous to clear analysis. Gripsrud (1997) notes that although the primary connotation has been that of being 'swept away by an external force', there has sometimes developed a rather contrasting sense of 'coolly and calmly regarding a river at a distance, possibly now and again distracted by what goes on in the immediate surroundings' (1997: 29). Clearly, these are two very different ideas of flow as viewing experience (Ridell 1996 explores this issue well).

As television, within a twenty-four-hour day, develops new times, rhythms, intensities, codes of visuality, modes of address, and channel optionality (see Chapters 9 and 10) many of the questions asked in the flow debate will continue to need attention. A look at the notion of flow and the discussion it has generated tells us much about the intellectual formation of television studies and offers several pointers about television itself which have yet to be properly taken up. However, the notion itself is almost entirely of historical interest. Rich though the phenomena are which it has been used to explore, it would be best if its legacy of confusion were not allowed to cause any further problems for television theory. Certainly, its rehabilitation would be a bold, perhaps imprudent, project.

7

Production

QUESTIONS concerning television production have always been important within criticism and research, although direct attention to production processes has sometimes been seen as a neglected or underdeveloped aspect of enquiry. With the possible exception of work on television news, there is not yet the richness of intellectual agenda here which can be traced in the history of work on institutional structures, programme forms, and audiences. Even enquiries into news production have frequently displayed too narrow an approach to popular knowledge.

One reason for the relative neglect and, to some extent, the intellectual underdevelopment of the area is the difficulty of gaining access to the production stages, of collecting enough data to be able to provide an analytic account and to generate and test ideas. Programmes, despite the difficulties of analytic method they present, are an exposed phase of television, their availability for analysis significantly increased with the arrival of videotape in the studio and then in the academy. Audiences pose more problems for the researcher, but not ones which are unique in social science fieldwork. To a point, structures of funding and organization (raising questions of institution, see Chapter 2) can be studied through the policy documentation which implements them or which they generate. Although production, too, is documented—it is after all a process firmly within the setting of institution—many of the questions which critics and researchers want to ask of it are not easily answered, if answered at all, by the schedules, memos, scripts, and correspondence files which trace its path, helpful though these are when made available. The extensive use of interviews to gain a level of secondary data and the methods of observational fieldwork (including where appropriate participant observation) to gain primary material are key procedures here, raising their own problems of implementation and of evidential validity.

Production is a phase within which different dynamics of television meet. It is *a* moment in a process but it is *the* moment of formation and this gives it a primacy no matter what transformations occur later (for instance, in the variety of viewer interpretations which a particular programme is given). It is a moment of multiple intentions, corporate and individual, however problematic these may be to recover. It is also a moment of creativity, in which various professional and artistic skills, framed by industrial requirements and constraints of resource and time, are brought to bear in order to get something on the screen. The interconnection with institution is obvious, so is that with technology and with textual form, including generic identity. The link with audience is more indirect, but is firmly there as a matter of strategic appeal based on producers' views about who will watch what on what channel at what preferred times, what they will immediately like, what is more risky, and how to project in publicity the values which specific kinds of programme offer.

The phase of production extends beyond the completion of the programme itself to include the carrying through of distribution and scheduling, increasingly strategic within multi-channel systems and requiring pre-publicity and final decisions as to target audiences, transmission times, and perhaps levels of advertising support.

Although, then, the complexity of the movement of television in society and culture is by no means fully determined at the production stage—a great deal of contingency and variation entering into the picture only afterwards —production practices inevitably serve to set limits, classify, emphasize, exclude, and build in ways which form the basis for much subsequent activity. In the next chapter of this book, I have discussed the extent to which questions of television consumption (as reception) have received strong emphasis in much recent study. It is not surprising that an argument about the relative weighting of production and consumption, and about the nature of the articulation of the two, should have developed. Briefly put, this argument has at its core two conflicting beliefs. There is the belief, widely canvassed in different variants and strengths, that a traditional emphasis on production has radically limited the explanatory power of enquiry in an age when the dynamics of consumption have been central to cultural change. Then there is the contrasting belief that only a retained focus on production relationships will provide an analysis of how television, underneath the 'democratizations of the market', continues to be related to structures of economic, political, and cultural power.

We can see from the above how the term 'production' sometimes carries the very broadest sense in media research, a sense derived from the classic tradition of Marxist analysis of modes and relationships of production in the development of capitalism. Yet it also has a more narrowly descriptive sense too, concerning how television programmes are put together. In fact I think it is possible to discern four distinct inflections to usage of the term. There is what we might call the *historical contexts of production*, indicating those general political and economic parameters within which television, along with much else, gets made. Then there are the *institutional settings* of production: the organizational and corporate sites of funding, employment, resources, planning, and making. Thirdly, there is what might be called, borrowing from the French usage, *production mentalities*: the dispositions, values, and working 'practical consciousness' of people at various points within the production process, having a range of creative, craft, professional, and corporate goals in mind. Finally, there are the *production practices* themselves: the particular skills and conventions of audio-visual construction and of performance which combine to make a television programme.

Within the history of television production studies, the incorporation of these four elements—contexts, settings, mentalities, and practices—has varied in ways significant for the kind of ideas generated. More specifically, the ways in which it has been thought possible to use one element as a route into others (for instance, inferring mentalities from practices) have had a strong shaping influence on the character of knowledge. They have compounded the research problems posed by the correlating of production with questions of textual form and of reception. For although television production has been researched for its intrinsic interest as a special, industrialized, kind of cultural practice, it has most often been researched in the hope that it will provide explanations for some of those features of television detected in its programme forms and its social consequences, including its presumed 'influence'. Among the questions which have figured on the investigative agenda of research into production are the following:

1. How does the source and scale of funding relate to particular kinds of programme and schedule?

2. What degrees of creative/professional autonomy are enjoyed by producers within the institutional settings and routines of their departments and companies?

3. How far is the production process a matter of self-conscious, reflexive decision-making and how far is it guided by institutionalized conventions? The potential tension between innovation and convention is a particular area of interest here.

4. How self-contained is the culture of production; how far and in what ways does it register broader aspects of culture and cultural change? This question can be seen as part of a 'society as source' issue, discussed by Phillip Elliott as distinct from 'society as audience' (Elliott 1972) and it may lead to other questions about the recruitment and training of television staff.

5. In what ways do producers see audiences, their expectations, and the responsibilities of media professionals towards them? This question will have different inflections in respect of journalism, drama, and entertainment.

6. How are professional criteria and role expectations formed and what are the working hierarchies within television in respect of job type, department, and programme categories? How are programme evaluations made and with what degree of intersubjectivity?

7. In what ways are changes in the production process due to emergent technology likely to change the nature of television programmes and of television as a communications system?

8. How is the programme, once produced, then positioned within broadcasting's market spaces? How do decisions about channel selection, channelling, publicity, and perhaps related merchandising get made? It has been widely noted that such decisions often impact back upon much earlier stages of planning and production, including the initial putting forward of a programme idea.

It can be seen that some of these questions fit more directly into an institutional perspective than others, which take account of institutional factors but have a concern with the local production process at a level of detail which exceeds the structural and organizational frames in which this occurs.

Many of the questions apply broadly, across the different generic categories, whilst others have a degree of generic specificity. We can draw here on a distinction which I have employed elsewhere, that between enquiry into television as public knowledge and enquiry into it as popular culture. The first thing to note about such a distinction is that, if applied rigidly, it reproduces a divided sense of television-in-society, and then a division of labour within television studies, which have too often had the effect of limiting research imagination in this area, reinforced by disciplinary prejudices. However, television's production of information, its protocols, phases, and practices, typically has a different profile from the production of popular series drama, say, or light entertainment. It is also work carried out under different kinds of policy framing and public expectation, susceptible to different kinds of criticism as to its adequacy and quality. Production studies of informational television, particularly of news, have often wanted to work with a distinctive agenda about the nature of informational sources, the criteria for televizable knowledge, and the transformative effects of the production process upon specific kinds of input (see Chapter 10 for more discussion on these points). Their approach can be seen as realist in orientation (although not naïvely so) in that they have looked at how elements of a real historical world, both as fact and as argument, appear on the screen. Production studies of drama and entertainment programmes, on the other hand, have most frequently wanted to ask questions about the cross-currents of aesthetic form, social value, and pleasure out of which programmes (variously conventional or innovative) emerge. Some of these programmes may be given considerable cultural space, as kinds of artefact with their own integrity and (initially, at any rate) a permissable degree of uncertainty as to audience size and response. Others will quickly have to satisfy specified viewer groupings within the framing of ratings competition. There is a necessary concern here with the imagination and with creativity, with a television authorship, which is different from the concerns of a public knowledge focus, even where there are similarities and overlaps.

It follows from the above that enquiry within the popular culture perspective will often be working with a less direct and more widely diffused sense of ingredients and recipes in the production phase than research on public knowledge programming, where the very existence of determinate pre-televisual sources (surveys, published sources, accredited experts, news agencies) allows a different agenda about televisual construction to be pursued. Given the range of variables affecting the look, sound, and cultural appeal of television drama and entertainment, it is also likely that work in this area will have a more extensive interest both in visual styling and in narrative, characterization, and affective appeal.

With the increasing development of infotainment formats drawing on news, documentary, drama, and entertainment modes, it might be argued that a division of the kind I have outlined is redundant. My view would be that the recognition of public knowledge and popular cultural production as distinctive imperatives within television still works well for the majority of contemporary programming and will be an aid in the plotting of those changes in production design and practice which follow from the further spread of generic hybridization.

Below, I want to look at a selection of studies in so far as they develop and generate ideas about television rather than simply describe what happens in production. These studies variously draw on the agenda of questions I have outlined above and engage at various points with the debates about conceptualization and method in production study. They are grouped under two headings—news and current affairs and drama—since much of the most suggestive work so far has been done on programmes falling within these categories.

Public Knowledge in Process: News and Current Affairs

Elliott (1972), already referred to, is a pioneering study in public knowledge television, carrying implications for study of the production process well beyond the specific genre which it investigates. In it, he follows the making of a seven-part series, *The Nature of Prejudice*, made in 1967 and transmitted on the Independent Television network. The intentions of the series were to explore in each programme a specific kind of prejudice (e.g. sexual, religious, racial) through a mix of location filming, including interviews, and studio scenes with interview and discussion. The format of the programmes was thus that of classic 'current affairs', drawing on a much richer depictive and discursive repertoire than that of the news, with a commitment to developing understanding through the exploration of subjectified opinion as well as the provision of information about an objectified, reported aspect of the social world (i.e. prejudice).

One of Elliott's more general findings, reflecting that of other studies in the area, was a picture of 'the media culture as a largely separate and self-contained system' (1972: 146). In particular, it was the formal and informal 'contact mechanisms' used by production staff to assemble material which, in Elliott's view, ensured an unwelcome degree of 'cultural repetition and continuity' (1972: 147). At points, he was able to contrast the production process of his chosen series with that of adult education programmes, noting the much greater authorial scope of producers in the former. Elliott's study, still rewarding in its detailed documentation of different production phases, emerges with a fundamentally pessimistic conclusion. Public communication is far from fully being realized in these programmes—the dynamics of the production process are too constrained by the autonomy of the media culture and the degree to which content is managed by conventional production recipes. Links with the public are speculative, even letters from viewers after transmission do not reach the production team, for by then they have dispersed and moved on to new projects—their own positioning within the act of public communication is abandoned before it can develop any reciprocal character, before it can acquire a sense of dialogue and accountability.

Elliott's findings, grounded in the specific observations of one series in the making, tend to support the earlier assessment of insulation in television's production culture made by Tom Burns. In what finally became a classic study, after a lengthy period of delay in getting clearance for publication, Burns (1977) carried out a detailed survey of working practices inside the BBC. The core of the survey is made up of interviews with personnel at different points in the production system. In a much earlier paper outlining aspects of his work (Burns 1969), he comments on the kind of institutional autism he found:

the producer must immerse himself in the particular unreality in which
his show exists, an immersion which demands involvement of a far more
extreme kind than we accept under the ordinary dispensation of a
'willing suspension of disbelief'. (Burns 1969: 70)

As in Elliott's account, the relationship of production to audiences is seen to
be simplified and often attenuated, 'the relationship with the audience has to
be reduced to the simplest possible terms' (1969: 70), and even in a situation
of ratings competition does not go far beyond 'the restricted use of Audience
Research figures to measure the size of audience and the volume of applause'
(1969: 71).

It should be noted that Burns's and Elliott's work was completed well
before the occupational culture of British television had to deal both with
the effects of heightened competition and the corporate requirements for
tightly audited cost-effectiveness which have impacted upon production in
the 1990s. As I write, the cultural analyst and scholar Georgina Born is com-
pleting her own detailed ethnographic study of BBC production in news
and current affairs and in drama (see Born forthcoming). In respect of my
own earlier categories, part of the value of her published commentary will
undoubtedly lie in what it says about settings, mentality, and practices during a period of considerable turbulence and conflicting imperatives within
the production culture of the BBC as well as within the national television
system as a whole.

I suggested that television news has been subject to production enquiry
more consistently and directly than any other sub-area of television research.
This is not surprising since news raises three related issues with particular
force, even for work within the broad generic area of public knowledge programming—the issues of sources, selectivity, and intentions. In 'gatekeeper'
research, initially looking at the organization of wire services for newspapers,
mass communication research has an early precedent for examining factors
of selectivity (see White 1950). Although still suggestive, the gatekeeper
metaphor radically falls short of indicating the complex news-constitutive
character of contemporary broadcast journalism, emphasizing instead a
more simple process of exclusion and inclusion.

In Britain, a major contribution to understanding television news-making
was Philip Schlesinger's *Putting 'Reality' Together* (1978), a study of BBC
newsroom practice based on a lengthy period of observation and over a hun-
dred interviews with news staff. Schlesinger described the everyday organization of news production within a 'stop-watch' culture and traced some of
the distinctively British ways in which the corporate viewpoint of the BBC
was informed by its relationship to the state and worked as a significant (if
unofficial and invisible) filter within the selective and constructional processes of daily news-making. In comments which refer back to Burns and
Elliott, he also drew attention to the ways in which professionalism worked
to intensify the in-looking nature of the journalistic community, reducing
the scope of reflexive appraisal and making any sense of audience often tenu-
ous. Schlesinger was pessimistic about the possibilities for change outside
'a restructuring of the place of broadcasting in British society' (1978: 272),
a view allowing little or no room for the kind of piecemeal reforms to which

internal critics of broadcast journalism have, not surprisingly, been most sympathetic. However, one of the merits of Schlesinger's account was the way in which it both located BBC news production within a specific framework of national and state values (particularly in respect of the definition and application of 'due impartiality' and 'balance') and yet presented a picture of occupational complexity and contingency, with different and sometimes conflicting lines of causality and institutional influence at work. This account placed question marks against claims of unproblematic professional independence but it also served to show up the limitations of the more functionalist accounts of news as propaganda which had gained credence in the 1970s.

In a recent overview of news production research, Michael Schudson (1996) usefully warns against the tendency in some studies to judge current practice against researcher-generated norms of TV news performance. These norms may never have been met in any country and are ideals which may raise serious questions as to their practicality and their fit with given configurations of politics, culture, and social structure. Too simplistically strong a sense of inadequacy may result from this approach, ignoring as it does the real history of journalism's development and the shifting forms of its market-related articulation with the political and the cultural.

The move towards more intensive and more carefully targeted publicity in many areas of society, public and corporate (see Wernick 1991), together with the emergence of single-issue pressure groups running professional publicity operations, has brought a growth in source-led news materials and affected the core processes of factual television production. Research is recognizing the need for more attention to both reactive and proactive sourcing activity. For instance, in a recent study Anderson (1997) documents source relations and their consequences for the development of environmental reporting and shows how newsroom-focused approaches to analysis may miss determinants of change active from well outside the ambit of professional journalistic practice. Again, Schlesinger (1990) has been influential in shifting the agenda of ideas here, criticizing rigid notions of 'where the news comes from'.

As broadcast journalism changes in response to new technology and to corporate reorganization internationally, production study will become a valuable dimension of research into the kinds of values and practices which emerge. Only with its aid can the relations and the disparities between proclaimed news policy and the particular sights and sounds brought to the screen be explored and debated.

Popular Culture and Performance: Drama

Studies of drama production, including popular series drama, have been undertaken with ideas also found in the investigation of factual forms (for instance, those about the political and social basis of thematic selection) but, as I noted earlier, they have also been informed by a distinctive set of questions about creativity and the play-off between artistry and industry within television. They have wanted to open up a sense of the kinds of negotiation, and perhaps the kinds of compromise, involved. To quote from Alvarado and Buscombe's (1978) excellent study of the making of the comedy private eye series *Hazell*:

> A model of popular television which sees it either as cynical manipulation or a straightforward identity of tastes between producers and audience (though there must be cases of both) would be, based on our experience . . . an over-simplification. (Alvarado and Buscombe 1978: 251)

The very high cost of much drama, particularly ambitious 'period' pieces, is a major factor in the production problems it raises. At one end of the scale there is the fast-disappearing 'single' play—a production group being assembled to translate a specific script to the screen. At the other end, there is the established soap, with its team of script editors, writers, and a regular fictional world to sustain within the parameters of viewing expectations. In roughly the same place, there is the long running situation comedy, again requiring continuity across characterization and a given spectrum of comic possibilities and comic appeal. In between, there is now a wide range of series drama and mini-series, exploiting episodic structure to different effect at different parts of the schedule and with both serious and comic intentions. These developing sub-genres raise, according to scale, their own quite specific issues of costing, creative opportunity, and the mixing of continuity with innovation.

Pioneering work on British drama serials, for instance Alvarado and Buscombe (1978) on the crime series *Hazell* and Tulloch and Alvarado (1983) on the long-running science fiction series *Doctor Who* has looked at how writers, directors, and actors combine their professional effort within given resources and requirements, working with distinct sets of professional criteria and kinds of satisfaction. Both the above studies contain excellent documentation of how their programmes developed within a broader institutional and corporate setting involving levels of bureaucratic control. They are both, to this extent, studies in occupational culture as well as of the making of particular kinds of television.

Later in the 1980s, two researchers produced an instructive study of the BBC drama series, *Boys From the Blackstuff* (Millington and Nelson 1986), a sequence of plays exploring working-class life in a post-industrial city. They drew attention to the negotiations, the delays, and the accommodation to different departmental interests which a major series encounters on its way to the screen. At one level, their study is an organizational one—the allocation of resources, the making of key appointments, etc. At another level, it is a study in the complexity of television 'authorship', highlighting revisions to scripts, the influence of the director in making adjustment to action and character, the discussions about what will work and what will not in relation to notions about the kind of impact intended, and the presumed dispositions and values of the audience. Although the constraints of the production context are revealed, placing the work as the 'product' within a schedule of available resources and deadlines, it is the perceived degrees of latitude, of space for experiment, self-criticism, and collective creativity which give the critical ideas of this study their originality and value.

There is some comparison and contrast here with a brilliant study of series creation in the United States, Todd Gitlin's account of the innovative police series, *Hill Street Blues* (Gitlin 1983). Here, the requirements of the network press down more directly and continuously on production development, even though the programme is working with a specific brief for innovation in themes, looks, and sounds. *Hill Street* was made by the MTM company, whose success was based on selective 'quality' appeal within given audience demographics and whose corporate history and distinctive socio-aesthetic profile has received detailed comment in Feuer, Kerr, and Vahimagi (1984). Gitlin pays particular attention to the way in which the production team work at aesthetic innovation, by a mixture of luck and judgement attempting to give their new show high generic originality without reducing its comprehensibility and appeal for target audiences. Of particular importance in the development process is the pilot stage, where the product moves beyond peer appraisal and is assessed for marketability with real audiences. The significance which the industry attaches to pilots, and yet the difficulties of using them as indicators for 're-writes' and for the making of good television, are presented by Gitlin within a largely negative assessment of the present effect of industrial imperatives on production.

Of course, for programmes that make it into a second series and beyond, the response of audiences is likely to impact back upon production in a number of ways. Success may increase budgets but it may also lead to even less creative latitude as the imperatives of sustaining popularity with a specific audience profile and within the terms of already indicated tastes become primary. In some cases, audiences may give programmes a rather different kind of cultural identity from the one which was intended, or programmes may be successful with audience groups other than those envisaged. In both instances, such a reinflection of the programme's symbolic values *in use* is likely to feed back into subsequent production decisions and into publicity and marketing. Julie D'Acci (1994) documents this type of cultural process well in her extensive study of the series *Cagney and Lacey*).

Although the kind of production values which centre on the success of pilot screenings have been slow to establish themselves in British television, it is inevitably a consequence of recent shifts in provision and regulation. Robin Nelson (1996) looks at the use of market research techniques in the development of the 1990s British police series *Heartbeat*, set in a rural community in the 1960s. He examines how the entire project was developed reactively from consumer testing, starting with basic concept choices for period, setting, and character. Nostalgia prompted by 1960s popular music was an important ingredient, leading to extensive use of hit-tunes on the soundtrack. A pilot was eventually tested in relation to different kinds of sampled audience groupings. In response to this, further revisions were made to script and treatment. In the context of traditional producer culture, such a consumer-driven approach indicates a new industrialized aesthetics for television drama in Britain.

Production is a defining phase in the social process of television which we need to know a lot more about. Ideas about production have often been too narrowly focused on specific observable practice within the institutional framework. Important though this is, a wider set of questions have to be asked about what I termed earlier production mentalities, the political and cultural values, and the sense of purpose of the people involved. Television careers, as studied through interview by Burns (1977) and Tunstall (1993), are valuable here, as indeed are memoirs and the more thorough kind of biographical work on those who have achieved fame in the industry, either on or off the screen.

There are many categories of programme for which little or no production study has ever been undertaken, particularly genres of entertainment, and for those where a literature does exist the work is often dated. In this situation, a good deal of inference and speculation will continue to feature in much academic commentary on television. Given the problems of sustained access, production studies typically have to work from limited entry points into the forms of cultural practice they wish to investigate and it is difficult to see this situation altering significantly.

Enquiry into production brings the academic agenda of what is interesting and important sharply up against that of the television industry. Except in special circumstances, a degree of suspicion, reinforced by the inconvenience of having academics on the premises at all, is to be expected. The more neutrally descriptive a study seems to be, the more pointless it may seem to media professionals. The more conceptually oriented or evaluative it is, the more disagreeable and open to objection it may appear. The rate of the change now occurring in many national systems also presents special difficulties for study, even as it makes it of greater value, by encouraging institutions to be even less tolerant to outside scrutiny as they respond to internal restructuring and to new corporate imperatives.

However, despite these problems, as the general debate about cultural production has become richer (in respect, for instance, of cinema, music, and publishing as well as of broadcasting), so research into television production is having to take with it a more conceptually ambitious agenda of the kind I outlined earlier in the form of key questions. Close description will still provide the basis for most studies of this type but, by itself, it is not nearly enough. What is also required is not only a broader understanding of producer cultures but more links, however tentative and partial, between production enquiry and analysis of the programmes themselves and the kinds of audience response they receive.

As television in many countries shifts towards more avowedly consumer-aware models, there is much debate about the extent to which the 'consumer revolution' in other cultural spheres has led to a real loss of producer power rather than to a different way of exercising it (see, for instance, Negus and Du Gay 1994 on the music industry). However, it is beyond dispute that an increased emphasis on market research and market strategy now figure in the production of television internationally. Future studies, no matter what their particular conceptual approach or focus, will need to recognize this right from the start in their thinking about what production now involves, what questions might usefully be asked about it, and how best to seek for answers.

8

Reception

RECEPTION, indicating the processes by which understanding and significance are produced by viewers from what they watch, within the shaping contexts and habits of viewing, was the most significant new focus in the television research of the 1980s. It has continued through into the 1990s with both a diversification in the kinds of enquiry undertaken and some signs of uncertainty as to guiding ideas, as I shall discuss later. It can be regarded as an emphasis on the consumption of television, the modes and the settings of this, but the way in which viewers engage with television and work its meanings, knowledge, and pleasure into their everyday lives raises issues very different from the consumption of material goods. In this respect, the notion of consumption can simplify what is at issue for criticism and research.

Essentially, the focus on questions of reception emerged from the cultural studies strand of work on the media, where it is in sharp contrast with the earlier commitment of that strand to an exclusive focus on the forms and contents of television output. Radically breaking with the kind of approach which suggested that depth analysis of television's texts could reveal adequately both what lay behind programmes (in terms of production contexts and assumptions) and what lay in front of them too (viewer influence), reception study opened out on to more empirical and contingent matters. The main strand of international television research, deriving from sociology, had a long tradition of paying attention to audiences through a variety of survey and focus group methods. Yet, however subtle this had become, in terms of its sense of the complexity and indirectness of influence processes and the active character of viewing itself, it had not shown much interest in how television's meanings were actually produced through the specific engagement of viewers with programmes. The reception perspective has thus had something to contribute here too, although the general rift between social science and cultural studies approaches has meant that there has been less dialogue between reception research and concepts and methods in this area, at least until quite recently (see the discussions on this point in Jensen 1996; Rosengren 1996; Lewis 1997).

By placing emphasis on the ways in which meaning is made and experienced by viewers, reception analysis necessarily develops an account of interpretation and its variables which is in some tension with conventional ideas of 'influence' or 'effects'. This does not have to result in a direct conflict of ideas, although for those theories of influence which work with notions of the direct impact of messages upon audiences (notions which can still be found, for example, in discussions of on-screen violence), this is hard to avoid. However, I shall suggest later that one of the most important points for progress in reception analysis is a deeper theoretical and substantive engagement with ideas of influence and effect, however critical the terms of this engagement may initially have to be.

Reception study, then, has importantly brought into focus a range of issues to do with processes of mediation, with television's interaction with the varied terms of public and private life, which were previously blocked by other ways of conducting enquiry both in cultural studies and in social science. In this chapter, I want to look first at how questions of reception were treated in the earliest television studies and then at significant contributions to thinking in this area and at some of the principal lines of enquiry which currently characterize it.

The Question of Reception in Early Research

In a very early study of how reality is presented by television, the North American researcher Dallas Smythe (1954) placed the functions of the medium firmly within an interactional perspective.

> Program material on television (as in other media) should be thought of as a group of symbols which serve as a medium of exchange between the mass media and the audience. This is a transactionist view of the relation between mass media content and audience members (and producers too). In this view of the communications process it is important to understand that audience members act on the programme content. They take it and mold it in the image of their individual needs and values. In so doing they utilize not only the explicit layer of meaning in the content but also innumerable latent or contextual dimensions of meaning. (Smythe 1954: 143)

In fact, the author is here on the way to making a case for the validity of content analysis, but the general terms of mediation which are proposed can be noted both for their acknowledgement of audience activity and their recognition of the 'latent and contextual' dimensions to a process which is essentially a symbolic one. There are a number of aspects to the formulation, however, which sound a different note from current research. The robust emphasis on content does not admit identification of specific questions of form, whilst the 'individual needs and values' which work to 'mold' content are still some way from an approach in which interpretative frameworks, cognitive and affective schemas, produce meaning. Nevertheless, the framing is far from being caught in simplistic, linear assumptions.

In much of the early research on television, however, the pressing concern with the definition and measurement of influence works against the use of any such version of transaction let alone an interest in specific questions about the constitutive character of interpretation. This does not mean to say that researchers regard viewers as simply passive objects whose minds are acted upon by images and sounds. In most cases, a variability of response is not only acknowledged but forms a main point of sociological enquiry —what kinds of people, under what kinds of conditions, respond in what kinds of ways to what they see and hear? (See Katz and Lazarsfeld 1955 for a major contribution to the development of 'effect variables' study.) However, 'response' is conceptualized as a reaction to an already determined message; it is essentially a post-message phase. The originality of the later reception studies is to pose interpretation as, in a sense, a phase of message production.

Growing out of the effects tradition, and in many ways positioning itself in contrast to it, was the strand of work which has been labelled 'uses and gratifications' (see the account in McQuail 1994). The intellectual design of this work is much closer to the terms of the Dallas Smythe formulation cited above although the primary concern is with the audience not with content. In an important collection which brought together work from this perspective (Katz *et al.* 1974), the emphasis is placed on:

(1) the social and psychological origins of (2) needs, which generate (3) expectations of (4) the mass media or other sources which lead to (5) differential patterns of media exposure (or engagement in other activities), resulting in (6) need gratifications and (7) other consequences, perhaps mostly unintended ones. (Katz *et al.* 1974: 20)

This sequence of research priorities places the output of the media inside a kind of social and psychological circuit. In this, media exposure becomes at least partly the function of broader social factors producing need-generating expectations. The output of the media then gratifies these needs and also, in the process, others too. Breaking with the linear model which starts with the text, it is an audience-focused view of the mediation process, hence the terms of what became a much-used phrasing along the lines 'ask not what the media *do to* people, but what people *do with* the media'. Yet this is still not a model which problematizes meaning itself, preferring to work with broad categories of content rather than specific programme items. Moreover, as has since been widely discussed (see Elliott 1974; McQuail 1994), its notion of needs tends to trap the range and the terms of its sociological enquiry within the categories and subcategories of a highly abstract, functionalist psychology. The posing of a circuitous process, although suggestive in itself, compounds this in application by creating in effect a self-contained explanatory system. The crudeness of certain notions of effect are indeed challenged, but alternative lines of approach to exploring influence are not suggested with any clarity and, as I have already indicated, issues of meaning become as marginal here as within most effects studies.

Signification and the Contingency of Meaning

The real opening up of the idea of reception in television analysis followed from work in British cultural studies during the 1970s. This work had always been informed by developments in literary theory and in the 1970s it had drawn increasingly on the semiotics of Barthes and Eco (see particularly Barthes 1997 and Eco 1972) in order to address the questions of signification and power which popular culture posed. Within semiotic perspectives, television texts were regarded as the products of multiple coding—the codes being at once both formal, systems and devices of sign organization, and contextual, conventions of public meaning, regulating understanding and affect. In fact, quite what 'code' meant became prone to confusion as usage extended to a range of sometimes very different phenomena (see the critique in Corner 1980), but the emphasis was both on the complexity *and* the systemic nature of meaning production. In the cultural studies version of semiotic analysis there was, right from the start, an attempt to register the pragmatic dimension of meaning and the levels of contingency which this brought with it. In a classic early account, often referenced misleadingly because, although it was an influential and widely distributed stencilled paper of the Birmingham Centre in 1973, it was only formally published in 1980, Stuart Hall (1973) sketched out the way in which television programmes as texts or messages were placed between two contexts of meaning. These were the meaning-structures of their encoding within the broadcasting institutions and those of their 'decoding' by audiences. This account therefore completely broke with the idea of an inherent meaning within the message itself, an idea which had variously been incorporated in much previous research, generating questions about which meanings present-in-the-text had, or had not, been 'received' by audiences with what effect:

> In a determinate moment, the structure employs a code and yields a
> 'message'; at another determinate moment, the 'message', via its
> decodings, issues into a structure. We are now fully aware that this
> re entry into the structures of audience reception and 'use' cannot be
> understood in simple behavioural terms. (Hall 1973: 4)

The terms in which it had to be understood were those of a process of the interpretative realization of meanings. This process involved the interplay between programme signification and the frameworks of understanding brought to bear on them by audiences. As Hall comments on the implications of this way of looking at things: 'there seems some ground for thinking that a new and exciting phase in audience research, of a quite new kind, may be opening up' (1973: 5). This a remarkably prescient assessment of what would still take another seven years or so to develop into the major turn television studies took in the 1980s.

Hall's paper outlines decoding in ways which would later become much discussed, developed, and criticized. Borrowing from the work of the sociologist Frank Parkin (Parkin 1972) on the different 'meaning-systems' of class society and their relation to the maintenance of power, he develops a preliminary typology of the ways in which viewers' own codes may relate, in various degrees of alignment or non-alignment, to the codes of the programme's making.

All this has a useful, exploratory, and suggestive character when read against the then dominant ways of thinking about messages in the social sciences, even if the degree of naïvety here has sometimes been exaggerated by cultural studies writers. When compared to the commentary of Umberto Eco, whose influential working paper on the 'semiotics of the television message' was published by the Birmingham Centre in the previous year (Eco 1972), it shows a greater subtlety and a more radical sense of the constitutive nature of interpretation.

However, Hall's account is rather limited by the reductionism of the decoding idea, which suggests one decisive and rather mechanistic moment of transformation of text into meaning. In fact, the conversion by the viewer of the images and sounds of television into significance, knowledge, and pleasure involves a much more diverse and complex set of significatory and socio-psychological events than this term can adequately indicate. Hall himself has since been frank about the modesty of his own ambitions for the paper:

> I didn't think of it as generating a model which would last for the next twenty-five years for research. I don't think it has the theoretical rigor, the internal logical and conceptual consistency for that . . . it's a model which has to be worked with and changed. (Hall 1994: 255)

He shows himself to be well aware of the provisional and sometimes polemical character of many of the working terms which he employs. His account was designed to make headway as part of a view of the circulation of television's meanings within the broader relationships of power and inequality to be found in a culture. How might one begin to think about the impact of public communication, the nature and influence of the messages of television, within conditions of structured social inequality? How did taking account of variant sense-making frameworks alter questions about the power of the media? Unfortunately, by treating it as a completed theory rather than a set of working notes, later researchers would sometimes carry the limitations of this original and illuminating sketch through into their own studies (see the discussion in Corner 1996b).

It is worth noting here a rather separate route through which ideas about reception came to be debated at around the same time. This was the literary critical strand of reception aesthetics associated with the work of European theorists such as Wolfgang Iser (1978), which was also appearing in a different form in the writing of American critics such as Stanley Fish (1980). The question of literary interpretation had for a long time provoked debate about textual stability and interpretative activity. Support began to strengthen for the view that literary readings and the practices of reading were at least as interesting a topic for critical assessment as literary texts themselves. The terms in which text-interpretation relations are discussed in this context often have a subtlety and complexity which compares favourably with the leaden jargon of 'encoding/decoding' (Eagleton 1983 provides a valuable appraisal). However, three differences might be noted between literary critical approaches and those from cultural studies. First of all, the concern within literary studies was mostly with the overall meaning of the text as an artwork rather than with the specific, local terms of social understanding. Secondly, the question of influence (*the* key issue for media research) was hardly an issue at all for literary criticism's engagement with interpretation, dealing as it was with minority, high cultural texts read mostly by trained readers, often within an academic context. Thirdly, there was little or no attempt to address the issue empirically. The debate was really one about the virtual and/or possible reader. The recognition of this might modify strategies for textual analysis and the assessment of other published critical accounts but it was an approach which could be pursued through broadly conventional forms of scholarship and speculation without resort to the vulgarities of survey study. It is interesting to find that work on interpretation in film studies often rather awkwardly places itself between this version of reception and the more empirical one deriving from the cultural studies decoding model.

Of those researchers in the cultural studies reception tradition who took up the challenge of empirical enquiry, David Morley has deservedly been the most cited and the most influential. His working paper 'Reconceptualising the Media Audience' (Morley 1974), was written for the Birmingham University Cultural Studies series six years before his study of the *Nationwide* audience (Morley 1980) which was to receive so much attention within media studies. The 1974 paper took its bearings from a range of social science and humanities thinking on interpretation although it was clearly Hall's encoding/decoding model which was the immediate spur. Morley was aware of the limitations both of the established effects and the uses and gratifications strands of media audience research, but he was also critical of the continuing tendency within cultural studies to engage with questions of media representation and ideology exclusively at the level of the media text. This was in fact to ignore both encoding and decoding moments in the Hall model, concentrating instead on the coded text itself, using semiotic perspectives in the more circumscribed, formalist way that they were being employed by literary and film critics. Drawing on his various sources, Morley pointed to a way of mapping audiences which would be sensitive to the complexities of meaning-making whilst providing empirical data on actually occurring readings, indicating not only their degree of convergence and variety but also, if less directly, their specifically social character and social origins. At the conclusion of his paper, he puts the position in these terms:

> I would argue that what is needed is the development of a 'cultural map'
> of the audience so that we can begin to see which classes, sections of
> classes and subgroups share which cultural codes and meaning systems,
> to what extent . . . (Morley 1974: 12)

Morley's substantive contribution was then to apply elements of the encoding/decoding model in an empirical project, using videotaped material with respondent groups to explore some of the variables involved in the interpretation of the BBC's popular evening news and magazine programme *Nationwide* (Morley 1980). Editions of this programme had been the subject of close analysis in an earlier study undertaken with Charlotte Brunsdon (Brunsdon and Morley 1978).

Morley's findings at the end of this small-scale but pioneering project were a good deal more conditional and circumspect than many subsequent commentators have noted (a tone which is continued most valuably in the brief retrospective essay of Morley 1981). In particular, he was alert to the very real difficulties in correlating interpretations with social group identity. This was essentially a problem which followed from the attempt to apply the typology of social class decoding positions suggested by Hall. Social class was an obvious variable to focus on in an enquiry trying to plot political and economic sense-making from news items. But the findings suggested that the fit between class position and reading was far from direct and that, working both within and across social class, other variables of cultural position and cultural competence determined the interpretative moves which viewers made. The map of the audience was more complicated to draw, the explanations of variability less directly traceable.

During the 1980s a small number of reception studies came to form a corpus of substantive work around which a large literature of commentary developed. The American cultural anthropologist, Janice Radway, made a strong impact on developments in television studies with her *Reading the Romance* (1984), a literary reception study exploring the role of romantic popular fiction in the lives of members of a women's circulating library. By getting to know these members well, Radway developed in her account a biographical depth, a subtle sense of personal, imaginative reading relationships, which suggested some of the shortcomings of an approach which proceeded entirely by group discussion and framed its questions in terms of the immediate experience of viewing video material. Unlike Morley, however, Radway was studying the often indirect and complex pleasures and uses of fiction rather than the specific propositional and evaluative sense made from news items. This involved a very different agenda from studies in television decoding and one which, in its own way, was equally as tightly framed and at risk of foreclosing on questions to do with the social causes and the consequences of interpretative variety.

Radway's project, in its reach back into the cultural setting of the acts of reading enjoyed by her respondents as well as into the specific meanings of the texts they read, can be more usefully compared with a strand of work, discussed later, which explores the nature of television's modes of address and appeal within the domestic spaces and times of viewing. However, similar guiding ideas are also to be found in Ien Ang's study, the following year, of viewers' responses to the soap opera *Dallas* (Ang 1985). Once again, the emphasis is on imaginative pleasure and its textual sources (e.g. characterization, narrative, setting), although Ang sets her account more directly within the terms of the media studies debate about ideology and popular culture. Once again, too, there is little direct attention to primary understanding, to the question of social comprehension, since the research is concerned with the level of evaluative response, with the reasons why *Dallas* is liked or disliked, judged as 'realist' or not. In some ways, Ang is further away from her respondents than Morley is to his, and certainly than Radway is to hers, since she uses invited letters rather than interviews as the source of her data. The benefit of this, compensating in part for the loss of a dialogic element and the possibilities for selective further questioning, is the more precise and considered formulations which are offered in the responses.

As discussion of studies like these developed, producing various attempts at imitation and modification, the issue of reception opened out well beyond the terms of Hall's model, to inform a number of different kinds of enquiry (see the more detailed account in Corner 1996a). 'Meaning' was being investigated, but at different levels, sometimes inadequately recognized as such. To find out that people differed in their views about whether a programme was 'good' or a news item 'fair' was one thing, to find out that there were significant differences in how viewers made sense of a programme quite another. 'Difference' was in some cases banally predictable, in others surprising and socially revealing, in still others evidence of a significant breakdown in television's factual or fictional comprehensibility. Questions about the reception of news programmes raised issues often very different from those raised by the success of popular fiction. Even within news reception studies, there was a difference between a focus on how specific items were understood in their local detail (as in Lewis 1985) and a focus on how the knowledge gained from specific items could be assimilated and used by viewers (as in Jensen 1986). More broadly, an interest in the interpretations made of discrete programmes, series, or even genres was not the same as enquiry into the general terms of television's involvement in the meaning and value system of everyday life and the home.

The Domestic Contexts of Reception

The character of television as a domestic medium is something which I have remarked on at several points in this book. At one level, this domesticity is self-evident and descriptive—television has been developed, following radio, as a system of broadcasting to the home. The television set has become a part of contemporary domestic furniture, first of all a novel marker of the modern—in Britain signalling the heady move of postwar popular domesticity beyond the 'realm of necessity'—but very quickly becoming naturalized as a cultural requirement, the absence of which for long periods produces an abnormal home situation. Television services and programmes have largely been designed to be transmitted to the home and both to fit in with, and yet also to exert a kind of benign regulation over, household routines. The spaces of the home and the use of these spaces in daily life have been changed by the physical presence of television just as the times of the home have been changed by its schedules (on the former, see the suggestive commentary in Morley 1995).

But television's domesticity extends well beyond these immediate physical and temporal factors, these grounding conditions, to inform the medium's more general character as a cultural technology. The recognition of domesticity informs critical ideas in relation to television across its whole profile (see, for instance, Silverstone 1994) and not simply in relation to questions of reception, although it is around these questions that much enquiry has understandably focused.

The phase during which television arrives within a national domestic culture (the availability of the television set, hired or purchased, to the majority of the population) marks a decisive shift in the meaning and possibilities of home life. Lynn Spigel (1992) has explored the new forms of often commercially initiated discourse within the home which developed around television in America whilst O'Sullivan (1991) constructs an oral history of the formation of a domestic viewing culture in Britain.

Television reworks the meanings of home life in modernity by developing new modes of linkage and separation between world and home, between public and private, often taking its cue from those established by radio (Moores 1993 brings work on both media together). Within the new system of culturally formative alignments, home space becomes permeable to the public world and the wider popular culture in ways which effect a radical change in both, as other chapters in this book attest. The possibilities for shared family entertainment allowed television to be canvassed, on both sides of the Atlantic, as an agency of family consolidation, but quite soon it was the potential divisions opened up between husband and wife and between parents and children which provided the main focus for comment, serious and comic. These divisions were seen to be both the product of conflicting viewing preferences and also, more deeply, the consequence of television's impact upon family discipline and attitudes towards conventional home culture (Spigel 1992 gives a social history of American developments at a level of detail not yet available for Britain). Certainly, no modern history of family life could proceed without recognition of the role of television as a device both of pleasurable and unpleasurable unity and of various kinds of alienation, evasion, and hostility.

Television was able more powerfully than radio to operate as a device of apparent transportation, in one mode converting the variability and risks of outside into an homely idiom, in another allowing the vicarious adventures of the magic carpet, with the viewer as traveller. In both modes, an aesthetics of the casual and the close as well as of the formal and the distanced was required. Television's mediations required a domestic register, an address to the home-dweller, to fit the scale and circumstances of their viewing. In the United States and now in many other countries too, this register was also a manifestly commercial one. Broadly, it was the address, however inflected by personal performance, of television-as-commodity to home-as-commodity. In Britain and some European countries, however, the domestic was more strongly overwritten by a deference to authority within a particular version of public service (British television was given to patrician tones well into the 1960s) rather than a commercial influence, although this quickly developed too.

Reception grounds television as a domestic medium in a way which not only confirms its everydayness, a device in a mutually modifying relationship with daily routine, but one which makes it also an everyday technology of gender. Television, across much of its programming, carries and exploits discourses of gender and gender inequalities in ways which frequently replicate uncritically the gendered values in the wider society and culture (as for instance, in the deployment of conventional versions of the feminine, of glamour and of the career woman). However, its domestic character and range of serious and light output allow for a more profound, routine gendering at the level of schedule and genre. It was around the figure of the housewife, and then the various forms of play-off setting up a contrast to this figure, that television's gendering was principally established. The history of scheduling cannot be understood outside of a process of alignment with the presumed times of home life and the role of women as keepers of domestic time (an alignment well documented in Paterson 1980 and Spigel 1992). A classic case of the housewife as pivotal to household viewing times comes from the research done prior to the BBC's launching of the early evening news magazine *Tonight* in the early 1950s:

> Any such project would have to be related to our assessment of what viewers would be likely to be doing between 6 pm and 7 pm. We made

inquiries. They would be coming and going: women getting meals for teenagers who were going out and preparing supper for husbands who were coming in. (Goldie 1977: 210)

The variables of schedule connect back into production, informing the gendered audience in terms of generic classifications. Of these, it is clearly soap opera which has been the most marked form of 'television for women'. The generic identity of soap opera is gendered across a number of ingredients in its aesthetic recipe (on its narrative organization, see Chapter 5) but, in Britain, it is its strong thematics of 'home', and particularly the roles of women within the family, which have been key defining factors. These are reception-related factors to the extent that it is television's broader domestic character which provides the quality of a coextensive, quasi-reflective fictional world, the ongoing, concurrent intertwining of real and virtual relationships and settings, so important to their success. Assessing the way in which the pleasure and knowledge of these imagined forms of domestic life impact upon gendered viewer consciousness, and then upon the real subjective conditions of domestic living, has been one of the primary issues in feminist discussion of the form (see the overview in Brunsdon 1995). It has connected with broader debates about television as a source of practical social knowledge and about the way in which the fictions of popular culture work both to extend and to constrain the contours of personal life and social possibility.

Television's domesticity is also recognized in the character of the regulatory ethos which is applied to it, despite the national variation which this shows. Home values, however vague and subject to rhetorical exaggeration, are a primary determinant of the taste boundaries within which television operates. They thus directly inform discussion of televised violence, sexuality, and 'bad language'. Here, there is the special case of television and children, where it is not only the forms of television for children which are at issue (although in both Britain and the United States these have been a regular point of controversy around questions of cognitive and ethical development) but also possible exposure to variously harmful elements of adult programming and the development of addictive, time-wasting habits. The distribution of responsibilities between the television system and parents has often been contentiously unclear but television, in most countries, has not yet been privatized to the point where no obligations rest on the providing bodies. The arrival of multi-set households, with children having a bedroom portable, worked to disperse the negotiated and imposed unities of 'family viewing' (on the character of both older and newer patterns, see Morley 1986), yet at the same time it set the conditions for intensified parental concern (just what *were* they watching up there?). The take-up of Video Cassette Recorders, loosening the nature of the alignment between transmission times and viewing times (itself a technology strongly gendered in use, see Gray 1992), provided the means for the even more radical shift of using the domestic appliance for material brought in from outside. Suddenly, the television set was no longer simply the front end of a service to be switched in and out of, it was an apparatus for exercising audio-visual choice, sometimes for options well outside of the range of television's homely aesthetic.

Applied technology, satellite and multi-channel cable, is now bringing a wider range of television into homes in many countries, gradually displacing the family viewing norm, creating a new domestic presence for Hollywood cinema, and, in some cases, introducing a level of sexual and violent depiction of a kind not previously in public circulation.

In my final chapter, I have given more attention to the substantive changes which are affecting the profile of television, nationally and internationally, and which will bring about a steady shift (and, I think, a degree of dispersal) in the terms of its domesticity. A more differentiated home ethos for television, less concerned with whole family units and presumed norms and more with the multiple consumption opportunities afforded by family members as different kinds of viewer, will design its forms of programme address for specific sectors. In doing this, it will tend to cut both across and under the level of the family itself. In many countries, the versions of generation and of gender which will then emerge from this redomesticization will move from an overdetermination by ideologies of the home to an overdetermination by individualized commodity taste. Versions of 'home shopping' will be part of this development, requiring new kinds of relationship to the screen as a device of direct, social transaction. Just what this all means for television's overall projection of the social, for its various factual, dramatic, and entertaining versions of how we live today, will indeed be a matter of urgent research interest.

The home base of television comprehensively underpins its identity as a medium, although it is grounded in the specific forms of its distribution and reception. Feminist scholars have often regarded it as a neglected dimension of television research, reduced to a descriptive fact rather than a political, social, and cultural dynamic. Certainly, its underrecognition within some of the more tightly rationalistic, processual models of traditional social science enquiry has resulted in a narrowed and skewed approach to many questions about television. On the whole, public debate, although it has variously deployed the domestic for partisan and corporate advantage, has not marginalized it. On the contrary, versions of home value, implicit or proclaimed, have lain close to the centre of many arguments about how the medium should be regulated and how it should behave. However, researchers have often found it difficult to make specific, modifying connections between the real terms of the domestic, as a structured setting for the experiencing of television, and other areas of enquiry. There has either been a semi-autonomy, the domestic as yet another aspect of television, or at times a degree of mutual suspicion and hostility between, on the one hand, the established agenda of work on the high politics of the medium and the analysis of programme-texts, and on the other, the more tentative mix of exploratory data and argument following from attempts at tracing the significance of programmes and programming within domesticized space, times, and subjectivities. This play-off—replicating at points that between the public and the private intrinsic to television itself—is likely to continue. However, more imaginative and inclusive frameworks of research, and an increased willingness by those funding research to go beyond the conventional protocols of 'reliable knowledge', would be valuable here, not only in the yield of information but in giving some now marginalized ideas and modes of enquiry a better context for dialogue and development.

Reception and the Question of Influence

In showing the fact of variant understanding and response in a wide range of researched instances and contexts of viewing, how have ideas about reception increased our understanding of television in society? They have certainly introduced a new complexity into thinking about the character of viewing, quite often displacing the idea of impact with that of interaction. What they have not done so far is to provide much by way either of specific social explanations for how variant readings are actually produced or firm ideas about the social consequences which variation, in a particular instance, might carry. Nevertheless, some studies have attempted to get closer to the causal nature of the relationship between interpretative variables and social group identity by holding a tight focus on selected themes being mediated. For instance, one of the most important findings of Jhally and Lewis's (1992) study of audiences for the popular American sitcom about a black family, *The Cosby Show*, is the way in which different sectors of the audience (across the categories white and black, middle class and working class, men and women) responded to depictions in different ways. The perceived salience and meaning of the class theme and the race theme varied significantly, showing lines of imaginative relationship to the programme which could be seen to draw directly on the ethnicity, social circumstances, and aspirations of distinct viewing groups. The authors remarked that far from diminishing the programme's ideological power, such variability might be better seen, in sum, to have increased it. It allowed the programme to develop popularity with large and disparate audiences through distinctive vocabularies of social meaning. The net effect was very different from the general promulgation of any specific message about integration and equality which the producers may have intended.

It is likely that such theme specific linkage between interpretative frameworks and the particular social biographies of viewing groups offers a more productive way forward in the researching of reception than attempts pitched at a more generalized level. Richardson and Corner (1986) looked at how views about, and experience of, unemployment informed viewers' local sense of the meaning and values of a documentary in which unemployment figured prominently. In a follow up study (Corner, Richardson, and Fenton 1990) the different frameworks used to interpret programmes about nuclear power were plotted in relation to viewers' political and pressure-group affiliations.

I noted in the introduction to this book that influence is one of the most treacherous and confusing terms in all mass media research. At one level, it is clear that television has exerted a wide range of influences on modern society and that its programming continues to exercise a degree of influence over viewers in respect of, for instance, the agenda of public debate, perceptions of celebrity, and images of other countries and regions. Elsewhere (Corner 1995) I have argued that the regular changes in the knowledge environment which television introduces can usefully be regarded as relations of influence, whatever the difficulty in plotting their precise direction and strength. Even the weather forecast may be regarded as influential if one accepts this broad interpretation. However, within the social science strand (and particularly the social psychological strand) of television research, influence has often stood for relationships at once far more narrow and negative. One might say that there has been an implicit hard-core definition of influence at work here. For some researchers, this definition is *the* definition and therefore of the kind of examples I have cited above would not be counted as truly issues of influence at all. The hard-core definition looks for behavioural change or a measurable reorientation of values and beliefs. It looks particularly for propagandist effectiveness where there is a conscious attempt to mislead or provide strategically selective information. It is interested in emotional and subconscious appeals, seeing influence processes as most often working non-rationally and (therefore) negatively.

My view is that this working definition is so narrow and carries so many assumptions (the term 'effects' perhaps carries even more) that a more refined vocabulary is needed, giving better focus as to level, kind, and scale of influential processes in relation to the hypotheses of empirical research. The real contribution of reception research is not to have displaced questions of influence (we cannot enquire into power without asking such questions) but to have made it necessary to review sharply the current ideas about its nature and variety and *how* it might work through television. In Chapter 9, I look further at how television's pleasures have been seen to bear on its abilities to influence viewers, taking the vexed issue of violent depictions for particular comment.

The development of enquiry into the reception of television by viewers has helped to form the agenda of recent television studies. It has raised questions about perception and comprehension, about kinds of viewing pleasure, and about the social condition of viewing which were often underrepresented in earlier work. Studies have become more diverse and have worked with different aims and ideas about what it is of most importance to find out. Methodological debate and an increased concern for more controlled procedures of data collection and data use have produced greater subtlety and focus and the promise of an improved conceptualization. The degree of emphasis now placed on reception and reception contexts by some writers has sometimes been seen to risk an underrecognition of other aspects of television. Certainly, the danger of reception studies becoming a semi-autonomous research field are now apparent and stronger integration with developments in other areas seems a prerequisite for progress in ideas and study. Both the more narrow and the more broad approaches to enquiry need advancing because our relative ignorance about the processes of sense-making from television's factual and fictional output is as great as that about the different conditions and circumstances of its viewing and its cultural uses within daily and weekly routine. However imperfectly, reception study has provided a documentation of what television looks like to ordinary viewers and of how it is watched, which is invaluable to research and criticism as a whole, vitally informing our sense of what the medium is and does.

9
Pleasure

To attempt to write about television and pleasure requires that connection be made with many different aspects of the medium. Therefore in this chapter I shall regularly refer to commentary to be found elsewhere in the book. Pleasure is, for instance, very clearly the product of the use of images and talk, it is often generated from forms of narrative, it is closely interwoven with questions of knowledge, and it raises specific questions about genre and about the nature of reception.

However, despite this, it seems to me to be useful to consider television and pleasure under a separate heading because quite clearly the giving of pleasure is the primary imperative of most television production and, with national variations, this has been true since the first services came on the air. In Britain, although there was strong continuity with the public service tradition of radio and its emphasis on information as well as entertainment, it was also quite widely recognized that television's potential most obviously lay in the massive extension of show business which it brought. As I shall show below, just how far television could be allowed to develop as a 'pleasure machine', and just what kind of pleasures were thought to be socially and culturally desirable for it to offer, were issues brought to a head in the debate about the introduction of a British commercial network in the mid-1950s. Here, the American experience of television pleasures was frequently put to service as an awful warning, however unfair this may have been to the full spectrum of American network programming. It is partly because, in most countries, television is given roles which include both entertainment and public information that the question of television pleasure is so different from the issues of pleasure raised around cinema, for example. Its amount and nature quite quickly become matters to do with the proper use of the medium, raising questions about national culture and about national polity too (including, in some countries, about public standards or even about political controls).

It is relatively recently that questions of pleasure have joined questions of knowledge on the academic research agenda and been seen to be interrelated with them in ways which are other than to do with trivialization. There has been a long tradition of seeing the medium as an agency of the culturally trite or even of cultural debasement. Asking serious questions about the kinds of pleasure which television gives and the way it gives them has occurred largely within, or has been influenced by, the strand of popular cultural analysis developed by the academic field of cultural studies. Within this strand, elements of popular culture (including the pleasures of television) are often rather ambivalently or uncertainly positioned. On the one hand, they are to

be taken seriously as part of an attempt to challenge the normative dominance of high culture and its hierarchical and dismissive attitude towards the
tastes of the majority of the population. On the other hand, they are to be
taken seriously because popular culture is to a large degree constituted from
the commodities of a major, multi-sectored industrial sphere, one which is
increasingly international in its operations. While the first approach suggests
an appreciation of popular culture (at times, a celebration) for its expressive
qualities and its relation to ordinary living and ordinary pleasures, the second suggests a suspicion of popular culture, largely for the degree to which
it reflects market values and is organized and sustained by conservative, corporate interests. Within this latter view, the pleasures of television may be
seen as diversions from the serious and the source of various kinds of dis-
torted or inadequate perceptions of the world. The precise play-off between
questions of pleasure and questions of knowledge varies considerably across
different studies, as do the criteria of assessment used in making judgements.
There is no doubt that in the 1990s, the increasing take-up of postmodern
ideas about pleasure, value, and social identity has led to more academic
writers seeming either to engage with popular pleasure on its own terms or at
least to take a far less anxious and critical attitude towards popular culture
as social knowledge. I shall discuss this development later. However, even
allowing for these new attitudes, an awkwardness around the analysis and
assessment of popular pleasure is still discernible in a good deal of writing
about television.

Given this awkwardness, I want first of all to outline a typology of television and pleasure, looking at some of the different ways in which the medium
is distinctively pleasurable. Much of what I say here may not be new, but it
too often remains implicit in discussion. Trying to confront questions of
pleasure directly will help to assess how they have figured in debates about
taste, quality, and influence.

Television and Pleasure: A Typology

■ Visual pleasure

Television offers an extensive range of pleasures in the viewing act itself.
Some of these forms of 'scopophilia' are related to the sense of liveness, of
being the onlooker to unfolding events, which certain programmes encourage. The enjoyment of being tele-present at a distant event as it happens can
still be a powerful one, inviting the viewer to look through the screen at an
ongoing world. Even where the sense of liveness is not present, the referential
pleasure of looking at pictures of things which are themselves pleasurable
either in form or in association is considerable and widely available in different genres. This (in one sense, realist) pleasure occurs for instance in programmes which feature natural landscape, attractive people, artefacts, and
places, spaces, and times which hold pleasurable associations (e.g. holiday
destinations, evocations of history). The pleasures of depiction are as wide as
the range of depicteds, and a matter of socially acquired enthusiasms (country houses, ships, aircraft, cars, kitchens, animals, etc.) which special-interest
programmes have recently become adept at satisfying.

But television has also developed its own, often dense, generically related
aesthetics, in which colour and the composition and editing of the image

combine with the use of graphics and perhaps of computer-generated effects to appeal to the eye. Image size and resolution may still mean that the visual pleasures of television fall short of the intensities of cinema (see Chapter 3) but the forms of appeal are well established. One might take, for example, the credit sequences of a popular drama series, the newer, elaborate styling of game show sets, the spectrum of programmes organized around music and travel, and the whole range of wildlife series exploring sea, land, and air. Using various recipes for realism or for a self-conscious artifice, television's different picturings both of the world and of its own creations are clearly a primary point of its attraction, a source of good feelings for the viewer.

They are compounded by the kinetic pleasures of seeing process and action, of watching things *happen*. These are pleasures which are exploited differently but strongly in a number of current fictional and factual genres.

■ Pleasures of
para-sociality

I noted in Chapter 4 how the para-social function of talk had been discussed by researchers interested in the kind of extension of sociality which television has brought. Talk with direct address visuals creates a relation of the sociable across distance which builds on the prior achievements of radio and adds to them the dimension of the physical person—appearance, facial expression, gesture. Television thus develops its own cults of personality. Such person-alities share certain characteristics of celebrity status with, for instance, the stars of popular music and film but they remain distinctive in the social rela-tions they enjoy with the public, relations grounded in their regular, familiar, informal address and their use of voice and face in an essentially domestic communicative performance.

Pleasure in the para-social aspect of television is dispersed across a range of channels and programmes, with fan cultures developing around, for instance, certain newsreaders, weather presenters, and game-show hosts. It is pleasure testified to, and considerably reinforced by, the appearance of stories about celebrities in popular newspapers and magazines, where aspects of their backstage life can be revealed and their self-presentation to the viewer thus gain more depth and resonance. The regular appearance of television personalities at public events (charity shows, fêtes, dinners) shows them being playfully invited into the real social spheres of specific groups of strangers, not primarily to do anything but simply to *be there* and to generate for par-ticipants the pleasing and privileged experience of seeing them in real life. There is sometimes a requirement for them to stay in role on such occasions, thereby heightening the thrill of a temporary alignment between 'on televi-sion' and 'in real life'.

■ Dramatic
pleasures

Television gives viewers regular and varied opportunities for watching enact-ments. Raymond Williams focused attention on this aspect of television, and its social impact, in his suggestive essay 'Drama in a Dramatized Society' (1974*b*). Some of these enactments are broadly framed within the current conventions of theatrical and cinematic fiction while others have a special televisual character. I have already referred to soap operas (Chapter 5) in re-spect of their distinctive narrative structure, character appeal, and modes of instantiating everyday experience and emotional life. Increasingly, docu-mentary, feature, and special-interest series employ dramatization or partial dramatization to increase the attractiveness of programmes. Indeed, the recent anxieties expressed about 'reality television' both in North America and in Europe (see Kilborn 1996 for a useful overview) are partly to do with the way in which entertainment criteria have displaced knowledge criteria in the formation of hybrid styles of factual programming. Television frequently attempts to be dramatic in two rather different ways. It constructs enactments both in its fictional and factual material, providing viewers with the opportunity of watching behaviours staged and organized especially for the camera and, in Aristotle's classic phrase, purporting to 'imitate an action' of some kind, real or imagined. It also frequently seeks to portray the dramatic in the sense of events of high intensity, strong in depictive impact. These two related meanings of dramatic, both now naturalized in our culture, are often confused. This is perhaps partly a reflection of television's implications for the available modes of cultural portrayal and the way they are thought about.

Whatever its genesis, gaining pleasure from watching enactment, from watching kinds of play-acting, is a form of cultural enjoyment with a long and global history. The imaginative appeal of drama, both as a temporary diversion from attention to real events and as an engagement (often deep) with a physical simulation, can be seen to have distinctive psychological features as well as developed uses as a vehicle for knowledge (see Chapter 10). The related question of the impact of dramatic portrayal (particularly when compared to that of written fiction) has often been raised where programmes have been seen to be controversial in one way or another (depictions of violence and sexual activity giving the most frequent cause for concern, followed by anxieties about kinds of distortion, including political). Television, then, has transformed the character and the scope of dramatization in the course of making drama a common cultural experience.

■ **Pleasures of knowledge**

By radically increasing the range of knowledge available publicly (if not always knowledge of a type meeting with conventional approval) television has also extended the pleasures which gaining knowledge involves. Sometimes dubbed 'epistephelia' (see Nichols 1991), such pleasure is an important element of the dynamics of human enquiry and the seeking of understanding. Quite frequently, of course, the attraction of gaining knowledge well exceeds any firm use-value which it can immediately, or indeed ever, be seen to have (in debate about education policy in many countries, the enhanced 'life values' which follow from knowledge have often been played off against more utilitarian gains). Popular literacy was a momentous step in the development of extended liberal education and television has widened accessibility still further. The public service tradition in many countries has often encouraged the pleasures of self-improvement, extending well beyond the direct advancement of knowledge to a wide range of increased delight in the arts, although usually involving some self-conscious application and effort. It has also often worked at the popularization of knowledge with great success—bringing programmes about, for instance, the natural world, about science, about history, literature, and the arts to mass audiences. These programmes might rightly be regarded as primarily informative but they have also brought enormous pleasure to millions of people for whom most writing about astronomy, the Roman Empire, the theory of relativity, the global function of rainforests or whatever would be far from pleasurable and often inaccessible. Television, as a popularizer of knowledge and an extender of the pleasures of knowing to vast audiences, is nevertheless assuming a role carrying with it a degree of dubiety and suspicion too, as the next chapter more fully explores. A trivialization of knowledge following from the market-driven character of much popularization has often been feared by critics of television, while some have criticized it for blurring together different orders of knowledge and placing kinds of gossip, anecdote, and whimsy alongside the product of serious enquiry with little regard for the procedures of knowledge production and the protocols of evidence and argument.

The long-standing popularity of quiz shows has led to charges that the public is being systematically invited to regard the memorizing of obscure facts as a pinnacle of knowledge, disregarding questions of context, conceptualization, and analysis for the theatrical intensity created by the possession and recall of discrete information within tight time-limits. However, given the way in which the knowledge requirements of formal education and of occupational and professional training affect the lives of people and their families in most modern societies, it is questionable whether television's pleasurable displays of knowledge as memorized facts have a significant influence on broader attitudes.

■ **Pleasures of comedy** The circulation of humour in a society through the popular forms and themes of the comic is an important part of the cultural pattern, particularly of public values and the desires and fears of private life. Factors of social division and social change across class, gender, race, age group, and region are strongly present in comic expression. Television has created a culture of public comedy which developed from that of radio and extended into new forms, including the situation comedy and a whole range of variants on the basic form of the music-hall sketch. It has taken the possibilities for satire and pastiche in a number of different directions and has contributed substantially to the re-emergence of stand-up comedy and acts based on monologic performance. It would not be exaggerating to say that the pleasures of television comedy have contributed greatly to the formation of nationally specific affective orders and to changes in these. Such orders provides norms for guiding, among other things, what is a matter for laughter and what is serious, beyond a joke. These in turn are based on the deeper structures of sentiments and feelings which underpin cultural and social values. Both the way in which certain themes move into, and out of, the realm of the comic (including public issues such as the portrayal of occupational groups and private issues such as those to do with sexuality) is very much a television-guided process, even if it also involves television reflecting broader shifts and trends in the culture of humour.

The formation of viewing pleasures in television comedy occurs strongly within the genres of children's and 'youth' television—both areas which have seen great changes in the last decade. The comic moods currently on offer here both reflect elements in adult programming and also signal emerging tendencies in comic sensibility. A distinctive play-off between 'enchantment

and cynicism' (Lury forthcoming) can be found within many new programmes, together with an increased tempo and sharp disjunctions of
sequence and mood. Across most areas of television comedy, the use of irony
has become more common. Combined with the more widespread employment of pastiche and with hectic, if not manic, forms of projected sociability,
this has been seen by some critics as part of a decisive shift towards more
postmodern forms of pleasurable viewing, although much of a more traditional character still retains popularity.

■ **Pleasures**   Television is widely used as a device of fantasy and even where the primary
of fantasy   viewing relationship is grounded in realist depictions, both fictional and
non-fictional, an appeal to fantasy is often present too. I am using the term
'fantasy' here to indicate a stimulation of the viewer towards scenarios
which are highly improbable for them in real life. Fantasy of this kind often
involves the viewer projecting themselves into fantastic circumstances, possibly by identification with depicted characters. If we look at fantasy not
just as a feature of programming itself (which it is) but as a form of pleasure deriving from the viewing relationship, then fantasy becomes a much
broader issue than a purely formal approach would suggest. Clearly, much
advertising plays with viewer fantasies, prominently erotic fantasies and fantasies of wealth, talent, and power. This element varies in its relation to an
advert's primary appeal and is often overt, so that a joke about fantasy is what
is really being communicated. However, criticism of advertising has often
wanted to point out the more serious exploitation of fantasy which adverts
involve, whether or not there is an attempt to disavow this by a degree of self-
consciousness and wit (see Williamson 1978).

Ostensibly realist drama may induce fantasy pleasures for some viewers
and, for instance, travel, food, and motoring programmes as well as documentaries and history series may contain strong inducements of this kind.
Questions have been raised about the particular fantasy pleasures derived
from watching the newer styles of 'reality tv', involving reconstructions of
crime and accidents and the use of surveillance camera material (see Nichols
1994). Such programmes clearly have a degree of directly referential attractiveness in their formats. A visual and kinetic pleasure (see above) is also often
present. But beyond both, there would seem to be an appeal to a level of fantasy too, perhaps driven largely by fears rather than desires, projecting the
viewer out into extreme situations, of violence and injury, yet also providing
conclusions of rescue and relief.

Consideration of fantasy cannot help but carry analysis into the area of the
psychodynamics of viewing, partly accessible to empirical study but nevertheless presenting special problems of evidence and argument. However, the
importance of fantasy to everyday self-consciousness and its presence as
an element not just of the private self but of the public and political self
too is only just beginning to be recognized in social studies research. The
everydayness of television's pleasures, so widely commented upon in recent
studies (see, for instance, Silverstone 1994; Scannell 1996) should not lead
us to ignore the fact that programmes stimulate viewing subjectivities in
ways which do not neatly answer to the categories either of knowledge or of

pleasure as these are placed within the normative schemes often assumed in studies of television.

With these points in mind, there is a final, perhaps looser, category of pleasures which also requires recognition.

■ **Pleasures of distraction, diversion, and routine**

The kinds of pleasure I have sketched out above are all variously specific to the degree that they derive from particular types of television programme content. Such content may be found through accident and happenstance as well as by purposive viewing habits. For instance, programmes offering the pleasures of comedy, knowledge, or strong visual stimulation may be encountered as part of a casual viewing session, determined by period of day rather than by programme choice. Equally, of course, programmes thought to be worth watching for one reason may turn out to be pleasurable, and even memorable, for quite another. There is an element of potential surprise, and indeed of cultural adventure, about television viewing which even its more tightly strategic targeting and the multiple cloning of market-successful formats has not removed. Of course, this varies radically with national system but I think it remains true for many audiences.

These issues connect with the broader experiencing of television within the domestic setting (see Chapter 8), in which the medium is often used as an easily available and familiar relaxant either after work or between phases of the day and where, simply, its not being work (either out of or within the home) gives it the comfortable and comforting values of a 'pleasure of the hearth' to quote Simon Frith (1983). All surveys of television use show a usage of this kind, which may nowadays be accompanied by regular channel changes but which may also proceed by following the schedule with a high degree of tolerance as to content. These are the broader cultural contours of being a television viewer, television as the take-it-or-leave-it medium, the available option for a break or for boredom, always there in the corner or (for many children nowadays) in the bedroom.

They are strongly gendered contours too, with the patterns of work in the home and child care giving them a basis in lived reality which has informed the development of the television schedule (see, for instance, Morley 1986 and Gray 1992 on home viewing patterns and the discussion of television's domesticity in Chapter 8). Within them, the regularity and repetitions of the viewing week, as part of a customized pattern of household/family usage, are themselves the source of pleasure, often carrying a confirmatory force which, like the pleasures of distraction, is delivered over and above the specific signifying work of programmes. Both in research and criticism, these broader and more analytically elusive pleasures have often been left out of analysis or prematurely pathologized, the latter tendency reinforced by the cultural guilt which many viewers feel about them, manifesting itself in a frequent reluctance to discuss such usage except in apologetic terms. Indeed, academic comment here can quickly become unhelpfully vague and speculative, but some of the more sustained forms of ethnographic enquiry have usefully attempted not only the documentation of these pleasures but their further integration into an understanding of television within everyday experience (O'Sullivan 1991 is a valuable attempt at approaching these matters historically).

Pleasure as a Research Issue

I noted above how television pleasure has only quite recently become the focus of direct enquiry, although it is a factor about which assumptions have been made from the very start of academic and critical interest in the medium. Unlike enquiry into television knowledge, it has proved extremely difficult to carry debate about pleasure into sustained empirical investigation. This is perhaps not surprising, given the difficulty in obtaining clear focus on a specific research object, but it nevertheless remains a challenge which might be more fully and imaginatively met by researchers in the future. Theories about the ideological dimensions of pleasure—its effectiveness in securing diversion, acquiescence, or even forms of political and social support for dominant beliefs—have been prominent in the critical literature, as have various ideas drawing upon psychoanalytic theory to explain the way in which television relates to fundamental human desire systems, especially as these are located within patriarchal, capitalist societies (on both, see the essays in Brunsdon, D'Acci, and Spigel 1997). I want to open up issues of research by considering them under three headings—the aesthetic experience of pleasure, the social relations of pleasure, and pleasure and influence.

■ **The aesthetic experience**

The key question here concerns the mechanisms by which pleasure is produced both in terms of significatory organization and viewing activity. At one level, this is a project of description and explanation, attempting to identify particular kinds of text/viewer interaction. At another level it is often evaluative, routing the debate about pleasure back to debates about 'high' and 'low' cultural forms and to the taste hierarchies which exist within television.

One relatively straightforward notion in accounting for pleasure is 'identification'. This premises a degree of viewer projection in which alignment is established between a character or kinds of action on the screen and the viewer's own subjectivity and its constitutive desires and anxieties. Above, I talked about this in relation to fantasy, although such a process can also be strongly realist in character. But sustained identification of this sort has both been seen as too simple a way of thinking about the play of fiction (see Carroll 1996) and also as an inadequate way of approaching the elaborate, self-conscious, and ironic pleasures which television now offers alongside its familiar ways of pleasing.

Roland Barthes's distinction between 'plaisir' and 'jouissance' (Barthes 1975), originally coined in relation to literary experience, has frequently been used in analysis of television. Fiske (1987) gives it extensive discussion. He is clearly drawn to the distinction because of its 'shift of attention to readers in their differences' away from theories of strong textual power, and its consequent supposition that 'the reader has some control over the production of meaning' (Fiske 1987: 230). Essentially, 'plaisir' is a confirmatory pleasure, resulting from engagement with textual elements which variously support social identity. 'Plaisir' has a marked cognitive dimension and is generated within the routine frameworks of cultural attention and disposition which are brought to bear in the acts of reading and viewing. 'Jouissance' on the other hand is a sensual pleasure, an articulation of the body. It is intense and carries a strongly erotic undertone, generating emotions which are at least temporarily out of control and not subject to the direct social conventions which govern 'plaisir'. It provides a shock, a thrill, a moment of social and cultural transcendence.

Barthes's commentary helps to make us more aware of general features of cultural pleasure as sensation and feeling, although its very generality makes it difficult to apply his terms productively in specific analysis. The distinctiveness of 'plaisir' finds an echo in the experience of many people, although it is more often at the cinema, the theatre, the opera house, and the concert hall rather than watching television that such moments are remarked upon. However, for Barthes (and then Fiske) the distinction essentially performs a polemical function. 'Jouissance' becomes a kind of utopian category, a category of escape, its experience providing opportunity for a temporary, personal transcendence of everyday necessity which gestures towards a better way of living and being. Exploration of the aesthetics of television pleasure needs to investigate further the phenomenological aspects of the pleasurable, but also to develop its study of the generic conventions and changing uses of image and sound which are pleasure inducing.

■ Social relations

Given the nature of the medium and the kinds of research it has generated, it is not surprising that attempts to relate viewing pleasures to social categories are more frequent than might be found, say, in literary, dramatic, or even cinematic studies. Television in many countries has both a unifying cultural profile, providing common pleasures which might be seen both to be informed by and to underpin public values, and a differentiating effect too, in which specific schedule slots or indeed entire channels relate to particular taste groupings. The official ideology of television in relation to these differences is often pluralist, tastes are different but equal, and this is an ideology which fits in well with the increasing need of many television systems both to optimize attractiveness to a general audience and yet also to develop programmes which appeal to specific groups of viewers.

Clearly, factors of gender, age, and social class figure strongly in the demography of television, and in many countries ethnicity is also a significant feature. Whilst there has always been a category of 'children's television', in Britain it was only in the 1980s that a clear sense of 'youth television' came to be developed by programmers and schedulers. The imperative here came from the recognition of a distinct affective gap between those in the 17–25 age bracket and older viewers. Of great interest to advertisers, viewers in the youth/young adult category might, it was thought, be appealed to much more successfully by a humour, style of sociability, and repertoire of themes tailored directly to their generation. More recently, and with a less obvious appeal to advertisers, programmes for the 'older viewer' have appeared. As television disperses across a range of channels, the opportunities and perhaps the commercial requirement for narrowcast programming and narrowcast pleasures will replace the traditional emphasis on broadcast modes. Already, the idea that television's strategy is to appeal to the 'lowest common denominator' in order to maximize audiences (an idea which has lain behind many criticisms of television's cheapening of public pleasure as well as charges of undue cultural uniformity) looks less convincing in many countries, including Britain. Of the new narrowcast pleasures, that of pornography has shown both a high degree of commercial success and a *public* controversiality which its placement within semi-private forms of distribution has not yet managed to displace. Clearly, the example of the internet takes this issue to a further, critical level of the conflict between public values and private pleasures. Many societies are now being taken into this conflict more deeply by a mix of technological and commercial innovation.

While differences in social class taste have proved to be the most contentious factor in debates about the pleasures of watching television in Britain, commentary and research on gender and ethnic diversity is developing in scale and recognition. Gendered pleasures have been looked at generically, with a particular emphasis on soap operas (Brunsdon 1981 and Modleski 1982 gave early attention to this issue with Geraghty 1991 providing a full-length study) and on the daytime schedules, particularly the studio-based talk shows (see Masciarotte 1991; Livingstone and Lunt 1994; Shattuc 1997; Richardson and Meinhof 1999). Work on ethnicity has included audience profiles and viewing patterns within a general review of television policy and programming here (Ross 1996; Daniels 1997) but also more focused ethnographic work on specific preferences and pleasures (Gillespie 1995).

In much discussion of the social relations of pleasure, there has been a manifestation of that ambivalence, mentioned earlier, where a wish to defend popular pleasures against élitist scorn, indeed perhaps even to emphasize qualities of resistance and of insubordination, combines with a requirement to recognize the capitalist commercial dynamics at work in much programming and the conservative values behind mainstream television culture. Given the public service character of their national systems (albeit that this is increasingly a residual feature), British and European writers on popular pleasure have generally felt it less easy to pass a straight judgement on television than many American commentators, assessing a more commercial system. Even the most pessimistic of them would find it hard, on the basis of present national experience, to reach full agreement with Mark Crispin Miller's 1987 conclusions about the medium's pleasures on the other side of the Atlantic:

> Night after night, TV displays a bright infinitude of goods, employs a multitude of shocks and teases; and the only purpose of that spectacle is to promote the habit of spectatorship. It celebrates unending 'choice' while trying to keep a jeering audience, all strung out. TV begins by offering us a beautiful hallucination of diversity, but it is finally like a drug whose high is only the conviction that its user is too cool to be addicted. (Miller 1987, reprinted in Alvarado and Thompson 1990: 319)

Nevertheless, this comment brings together elements of a critique of the pleasures of television, indeed a verdict on its general cultural status, which has been made internationally. It is a critique which is rooted in observations about content but which finally fears the kind of culture which the medium encourages or even produces. It is not a direct condemnation of audiences, but their involvement in television's version of the popular is both strongly implicit and unflattering. Attempting to go beyond the *impasse* of judgements like this towards the terms of a more specific, and perhaps sympathetic, understanding or at least the terms of realizable alternatives, has been the goal of many recent studies wanting to explore television pleasure in relation to broader questions of social value (see, for example, the essays in Lusted and Geraghty 1997).

■ **Influence**   Viewing pleasures have been related to ideas of influence in a number of ways. It has been widely argued that one of the consequences of much 'pleasing' is to distract and divert, such that important political and social questions are not given viewers' sustained engagement. Television, on this account, acts within the terms of the classic 'bread and circuses' formula, keeping the populace happily uncritical (the title of Neil Postman's anti-television polemic, *Amusing Ourselves to Death* (1987), carries a strong implication of this kind).

A more fundamental line of influence than diversion is the use of pleasure in securing unreflective support for particular political and social positions. The use of humour to reinforce prejudice, the use of strongly nationalist aesthetics (including music and dance) to promote xenophobia, the use of various types of sexual objectification, and the depiction of violence (including sexual violence) in ways which encourage kinds of spectator enjoyment are all examples of influence working *through* pleasure.

Both sexual objectification for pleasure and the depiction of violence raise questions about the relationship between the realm of fantasy and the realm of real values and attitudes. The debate about pornography and screen violence often turns on how these realms are seen to be interconnected (see McNair 1996). In the much-cited formulation 'pornography is the theory, rape is the practice' the connection is quite firm and direct. A number of behavioural psychologists have worked with a similar, if differently conceptualized, sense of how fantasy pleasures impact upon real attitudes and behaviour (for instance, through the triggering of emotional subsets, particularly in 'unstable' personalities). That pleasure in depicted sexuality will have an impact upon sexual subjectivity and socio-sexual perceptions more generally seems indisputable. At one level, this is a matter of how the attractive and the sexy are socially coded. At another level, it is about the use of pornography for sexual gratification. Increasingly, specialist television channels are combining with the well-established video sector to supply this usage. The middle- and long-term impact of pornographic pleasures on real sexual relationships is disputed—a welcome stimulation of appetite in one view, a serious distortion of human values and the possibilities for mature sexual satisfaction in another. This is a strongly gendered issue of course, since by far the majority of pornographic portrayals, on television as elsewhere, are aimed at men and depict women very much in roles which frame their sexuality within the terms of 'whore', 'slave', and 'victim'. Such negativeness becomes even more disturbing when implied or explicit violence is introduced into pornographic scenarios, carrying the terms of the portrayal well beyond acceptable real-life practices in a way which more conventional pornographic imagery, whatever its fetishistic and reductive character, does not.

When we turn to the full range of depicted violence on television, then the question of getting pleasure from the witnessing of dramatic imitations of actions which in real life would, normatively, provoke disgust, outrage, and horror is raised most provocatively. In Corner (1995) I discussed the cultural paradox which is apparent in a situation where the widespread circulation of images of violence is allowed but deep concern is shown about nearly all images of explicit sexuality. That which is generally regarded as bad behaviour, if not criminal behaviour, in real life is, in depicted form, a staple of popular entertainment, whereas that which is regarded as an enjoyable part of common human experience is, in depicted form, the object of intensive censorship.

In looking at the pleasures of watching violence, we have to take account, among other things, of the way in which violence provides 'action values' upon which many popular narratives depend for their generation of excitement. Action values are the dramatic and kinetic satisfactions obtained by watching physical activities where the energy, scale, and spectacular qualities of the depiction are prominent. Westerns, adventure stories, thrillers, and many crime narratives are strong in action values (e.g. car chases, escapes, ambushes, raids, fights) and also often in graphic scenes of violence. This use of violence (often misleadingly described as 'gratuitous' when in fact its dramatic function is central and sometimes generically defining) is widespread in the culture and can to some extent be differentiated from depictions of violence where the entertainment function is secondary to some more serious dramatic exploration of historical, social, or psychological themes. In earlier work, I have drawn on a distinction between 'turn off' violence and 'turn on' violence to explore a differentiation between televised depictions which seek primarily to give pleasure from the depiction (the fight, the raid, the crash, etc.) and those which intend primarily to draw the viewer into a non-pleasurable form of engagement, including the production of shock and disgust. Giving the viewer a harrowing rather than enjoyable experience might well be the aim of a director filming, for instance, a scene of torture in a drama about a political coup in Latin America.

The idea that getting pleasure from watching depicted violence is, by itself, a bad thing is hard to sustain in the face of its sheer normalization across so many areas of contemporary culture—from children's cartoon and Westerns through to war stories and the subgenres of the thriller and the adventure series. Generally, of course, television systems have had to be more careful in their regulation here, recognizing the possibility of offence to general public taste, than has cinema, but the new multi-channel context has radically increased the opportunities for television to carry the stronger forms of cinematic violence. The way in which 'turn on' violence seeks to generate pleasure vary radically, a fact not always sufficiently recognized in the research literature. Where the element of stylization and play is foregrounded (as it clearly is, for instance, in cartoons, in many Westerns, and in certain kinds of thriller) then concern does not seem to be so great as in those cases where a high degree of graphic realism is introduced—giving the violent scenes themselves a physically explicit character (e.g. damage to parts of the body, the experiencing of pain, bleeding, obvious distress). Just how far the enjoyment of such scenes has a pathological character, not retrieved by talk of play, or how far we are dealing with an aspect of modern sensibility in which there is an adequate disjunction between the ethical frameworks used in reading the scenes and those used in reading reality has been the subject of much dispute (see Miller and Philo 1996; Barker and Petley 1997; and Hill 1997).

Once again, it is useful to remind ourselves that it is not at all the seriousness of the violence as it would be measured in real life that is at issue here. To assume this is a frequent mistake in arguments about televised violence and can be found in some research on it. It is, rather, the manner in which the viewer is invited to watch the violence. The depiction of a murder can pose far less of a problem than a scene of a mugging. Inevitably, scenes involving sexual violence and torture have provoked the most concern, many critics holding the view that *any* level of pleasure taken from scenes of this kind is quite unacceptable in its appeal to, and encouragement of, violent desire even where this desire may be argued to remain within the realm of fantasy. This is an area which will clearly receive much more attention from a number of research perspectives. One of the challenges for those who express fears about influence is the tighter evidencing of the mechanisms through which it works. Clearly, claims about violent depictions producing a disposition to engage in violent behaviour need the firmest empirical support, while arguments about less direct changes to attitudes and emotions could also benefit from clearer conceptualization and analysis (Chapter 8 considers this point further).

In looking at how pleasure is related to influence in television studies, its function in advertising should be noted too, if here only briefly. Much television advertising works by different strategies of 'value transfer', by which pleasing things in the advert (e.g. features of design, settings, people, acts, clothes, possessions) effect a positive evaluation of the product. However ironic and self-conscious advertising has now become, the production of pleasure around the product and thereby potential pleasure *in* the product is often a fundamental aim. Advertising as an extremely well-funded desire machine, variously emphasizing, distorting, displacing, and effacing, has been a focus of much television criticism and research (useful discussion can be found in Leiss, Kline, and Jhally 1986; Wernick 1991; Davidson 1991; and Goldman 1992). It raises some of the questions of fantasy, play, and reality values which I have discussed above in relation to sexual and violent depictions, while at the same time ranging across a broader social canvas, offering vicarious pleasures of a less intense and more everyday kind (for instance, of home, of family life, of recreation, of friendship, and of holidays).

Television Pleasures, Taste, and Quality

I want to conclude this review of how questions of pleasure figure in criticism and research by looking briefly at aspects of the debate about television quality. Quality has been an important issue in the formation of British broadcasting policy in the 1990s and has appeared in debates about national television systems throughout Europe and beyond (Brunsdon 1990; Mulgan 1990; Schroder 1992; and Corner, Harvey, and Lury 1994 reflect variously on the use of the term). Much to do with the debate about television quality turns on shifts in the regulation, funding, and institutional character of the medium—'quality' signals a concern with defining more clearly what, in television terms, can be assessed as a good product and thereby used as a marker in both public and corporate audits of the industry. The usage here is essentially one derived from the vocabulary of management theory, where ideas about quality control and procedures for quality development have had a widespread application in both the public and private sector as part of corporate restructuring and the drive to higher efficiency and productivity. There is therefore a strong element of industrial standards in the debate about the achievement and maintenance of quality television. These standards concern, for instance, technical and craft production values, delivery of schedules in line with stated company policy, and responsiveness to the demands of those audiences indicated in the public or commercial remit of the channel. Yet argument about quality inevitably has a tendency to slip quite quickly from the more objectifiable and auditable aspects of how television performs to the more subjective ones—to questions of generic preference, to class, gender, and age-related variations in cultural taste, and to different ways of relating to the popular. Factual programming certainly raises these issues (for instance, about the format, treatment, and tone of news programmes; about the topics and approaches of documentary) but, for obvious reasons, it is drama and entertainment which manifest them most sharply.

It is interesting to note the following comments about popular taste, made just after the introduction of British commercial television in 1955. They were offered by one of the leading executives of the new system which had broken the BBC monopoly in the declared interests of popularity and choice:

> If one gave the public exactly what it wanted it would be a perfectly appalling service . . . It is quite obvious that the educational standard of this country is deplorable . . . The overwhelming mass of the letters we get are illiterate . . . all they write for are pictures of film stars, television stars, or asking why there are not more jazz programmes, why there cannot be more programmes of a music-hall type. (Norman Collins, cited in Williams 1962: 63)

This comment, extraordinary for a new champion of commercial television, clearly shows a gap between what are judged to be the tastes of the popular audience and the taste level at which it is thought fit to provide a television service. Perceived market demand for certain pleasures is overridden by the standards of the supplier, consumer values are subordinate to those of the producer. Not surprisingly, other public figures involved in the mid-1950s debate about national television in Britain took a different view of the audience's relation to broadcasters. Selwyn Lloyd, a Conservative Party spokesman on broadcasting, saw the matter in terms of a 'fair' play-off between knowledge and pleasure underwritten by principles of democratic rights:

> If people are to be trusted with the franchise, surely they should be able to decide for themselves whether they want to be educated or entertained in the evening. (Lloyd 1951: 205)

If we then jump forward to 1989, with British broadcasting on the edge of another, equally radical, phase of transformation, here is Rupert Murdoch addressing the Edinburgh Television Festival:

> Much of what passes for quality on British television really is no more than a reflection of the values of a narrow élite which controls it and which has always thought its tastes are synonymous with quality.
> (Murdoch 1989)

In this comment, from one of the world's most powerful television entrepreneurs, the market liberalism underlying his whole project is linked directly with a liberation from oppressive 'élite' values. His attack on the conventional criteria of 'quality' brings out sharply a tension between publicly protected cultural values and the popular pleasures of cultural markets which has been present in discussion of television in Britain since the 1950s but which is now being played out in a quite new context of programme provision and viewer expectations (see Chapter 11 for the international outlines of this). New social relations of television pleasure and perhaps new terms for discussing taste are entailed by the shift.

Television criticism and research, having only quite recently recognized the full extent to which questions of pleasure are implicated in many arguments ostensibly about something very different—for instance, about knowledge, information, the supporting of citizenship, provision for minority groups, and the relation of the national to the international—will now have to give its attention to a much more complex and extended pattern of tastes and practices of taste formation and satisfaction

10
Knowledge

THE question of television's impact upon popular knowledge, a question both about processes and their consequences, has been the most frequently asked question in television research. However, it has been asked in such a wide variety of ways that the degree of continuity, coherence, and development across different research perspectives has been low. Questions of knowledge feature significantly in the long tradition of influence and effects research, conducted principally within the terms of the social sciences (see my comments on this in the introductory chapter). They are also directly at issue in that broad range of work which has used the notion of ideology as a key concept in exploring the relationship between television and the political and social order.

In this chapter, I want to look at the ways in which questions about knowledge and television have been posed. While some are concerned with the range and quality of knowledge made available through television, others are more interested in the processes of knowing—what is distinctive about television as a *medium* of knowledge? What is the nature of the cognitive experience which it offers when compared, say, to reading a newspaper? Many studies have looked at knowledge exclusively in terms of factual programming, but a recognition of the way in which knowledge functions are also performed by drama and entertainment genres is now more widely being shown.

Among critics and researchers, anxiety about the potential of television to hinder the formation and communication of knowledge (and thus to limit the scope and efficiency of the public sphere, see Chapter 2) far outweighs any sense of its positive capacities either in presenting knowledge in new ways or in extending the range of the knowledgeable in different fields. I shall consider at some length those who make a positive assessment of the medium, but first I want to divide the very large number of those who do not into three broad categories of approach.

Three Types of Badness

■ Misselection

By this, I mean those studies which, theoretically and analytically, attempt to show the ways in which television acts as a gatekeeper, admitting only a selection from available knowledge to receive the endorsement and amplification of television. This may be seen to operate in respect of political and social knowledge (news and current affairs) but also in respect of artistic, historical, and scientific areas of knowledge too. Television is, of course, *necessarily* selective as a medium but if its selections are judged to be unduly narrow, supportive of a limited range of political positions, filtering out that which is challenging and critical of current social convention, why might this be? There are two possible answers to this question and they can be offered either separately or in combination. First of all, selection can be seen as a function of bureaucratic control. Directly or indirectly, in most countries the state exercises a regulatory function over the institutions of television (see Chapter 2) and this produces a selectivity which is likely to support broadly official positions in respect, for instance, of national history, ethnic balance, domestic and social propriety, international affairs, scientific development, defence policy, etc. Undoubtedly, in some countries, this controlled selectivity is present at a very high and explicit level. Elsewhere, it is less pronounced or more covert.

Another possible reason for selectivity is less motivated and planned. It is a consequence of television as a commodified system, subject to market structures. Within these structures, perceptions of commercial safety and risk will inform decisions as to what kinds of programme are developed and what are not. It will also inform the kinds of knowledge which are drawn on in making these programmes. Even in news and current affairs, there will be criteria for what makes a good news story which will exert an influence on the news agenda, even if this is also shaped by other factors too. In conditions of strong market competition, it is often argued, the real choice of knowledge made available for the viewer, in contrast to the claims made for its increase, may be constrained. This happens as the requirement for profitability encourages programming to work from the safer kinds of core material, reflecting established dispositions and prejudices.

Assessment of the commodification effect on selectivity is complicated. First of all, in many national systems, commercial dynamics have emerged in opposition to state controls, often leading to a situation which, initially at least, is one of relative liberalization. In other systems, the commercial sector has displaced a form of public provision which, whilst it might (as in Britain) have been open to accusations of an imposition of values, nevertheless frequently worked with principles of public accountability and the public good rather than of selective market advantage. Secondly, as the various vectors of deregulation and multi-channel competition in international television work their way through national systems, the kinds of spaces opened up and closed down for the circulation of types of knowledge cannot always confidently be predicted. For instance, in many countries, some minority audience groups have been served better through commercial cable provision than through major terrestrial networks. What has been seen to be profitable has not necessarily meant a reduction to the terms of a *mass* audience—indeed, quite the opposite position has been more typical of the market logics of the 1990s.

■ **Misprestentation**   This is essentially a development from misselection. However, instead of emphasizing the *content* of knowledge on television, the stress here is on the *form* it takes. Typically, a critique is made of the emphasis on pictures, the brevity of contextualization, the strongly narrativized and personalized devices employed across a range of genres. The focus on shortcomings in the presentation of knowledge on television (news, science programmes, natural history series, history series, etc.) follows much more often from ideas about commodification than from ideas about direct bureaucratic control. It is thus the market character of television which is seen to produce distortive effects, although a linkage between this and certain interests of the state may also be proposed. Rather than any directly propagandistic strategies, however, it is television's seductive, populist appeal, its *apparent* character as the agency of democratic knowledge and pleasure in combination with its *real* inadequacies, which attracts critical attention. That body of work on television which uses the notion of ideology (variously discussed at points throughout this book but see Hall 1977 for an influential essay) has often given particular attention to questions of mispresentation, although it has been concerned with misselection too (both of the bureaucratic control and commodification variety). The various realisms of television portrayal (see Chapter 3) have perhaps been identified as the most significant element of ideological misrepresentation, conferring a naturalness and obviousness to the visually portrayed world which displaces or mystifies relations of power and inequality and legitimates dominant power groups (Thompson 1990 gives a useful, general account).

■ Misknowing: debasement of the knowledge process

A further criticism of television's knowledge functions, one heard more often in the United States than elsewhere, concerns neither the content nor nor the form of knowledge itself. It concerns instead the actual processes of perception, cognition, and understanding. Television's conventions of depiction and exposition are seen to have led to a deterioration in the knowledge-processing capacities of the public. There has, in this view, been a general 'dumbing down' brought about by television, an atrophying of critical intellectual skills, a reduction in attention spans, a requirement to be 'diverted' rather than challenged, which has now established itself as a cultural norm. The American writers Jerry Mander and Neil Postman have produced classic works of polemic along these lines, with a convergent general judgement issuing from their rather different kinds of appraisal of epistemological consequences (Mander 1978; Postman 1985). Postman's *Amusing Ourselves to Death* achieved widespread recognition as a book which was bold enough to identify the true dangers of television, lying beyond the routine arguments about specific contents and forms. The British weekly, *New Society*, caught a more general response to the book when it noted in its review 'Postman illuminates something ominous: a society being rendered unfit to remember or to think, taking its ignorance as knowledge.' Other writers, before and since, can be seen to be pursuing ideas of misknowing, variously drawing on psychological and sociological perspectives in so doing. Like Postman, such writers often draw an explicit contrast between the epistemic order encouraged by television and that encouraged by print.

The Knowledge Potential of Television

I noted above how heavily the assessment of television's knowledge functions is weighted towards pessimistic and critical opinion. Nevertheless, there are a number of commentators who have attempted to make a more positive case. This may not necessarily signal a disagreement with those offering critiques so much as experience of a different kind of television system.

Of those writers who have commented generally on the medium's knowledge functions, Marshall McLuhan and Joshua Meyrowitz repay a closer consideration here. McLuhan remains a key figure in the history of ideas about media and mediation. Indeed, as I noted in my introductory chapter, his intellectual concerns and his approach have had something of a revival as an agenda of enquiry influenced by postmodernist thinking has returned to many of the broad themes of technological transition, sensory experience, and cultural order which he pursued in his own essays (to some extent drawing on the earlier ideas of another influential thinker about technology, communication, and culture—Harold Innis, see Innis 1951). Meyrowitz, although he too is concerned with general tendencies, has a grounding sociological interest in the specifics of change in the community.

McLuhan's assessment of the revolution in popular knowledge which television has brought about is overdetermined by his primary interest in the media as extensions of the human senses. His commentaries are above all characterized by a feeling of excitement about change, a registering of broad and fundamental shifts in culture, which more often imply a positive judgement than make it explicit (as a young scholar, he had also been influenced by the Cambridge critic F. R. Leavis, whose own concern about the future of social community within contemporary economic and cultural development was far more pessimistic). However, some passages carry stronger implications than others. Here is McLuhan in the introduction to his classic collection of essays, first published in 1964, *Understanding Media*:

> After three thousand years of specialist explosion and of increasing specialism and alienation in the technological extensions of our bodies, our world has become compressional by dramatic reversal. As electronically contracted, the globe is no more than a village. Electric speed in bringing all social and political functions together in a sudden implosion has heightened human awareness of responsibility to an intense degree. It is this implosive factor that alters the position of the Negro, the teen ager, and some other groups. They can no longer be *contained*, in the political sense of limited association. They are now involved in our lives, as we in theirs, thanks to the electric media. (McLuhan 1973: 12–13)

This recording of what is seen as a largely benign change is reinforced a few lines later:

> The aspiration of our time for wholeness, empathy and depth of awareness is a natural adjunct of electric technology. The age of mechanical industry that preceded us found vehement assertion of private outlook the natural mode of expression. (McLuhan 1973: 13)

In many ways, this perspective reverses the emphasis of critics like Postman, who see fragmentation where McLuhan sees connection, shallowness where he sees depth, and increasing individualism where he sees the making of new community. And far from seeing a freedom from political containment, many critics of television would point to the increase in subtle and effective possibilities for control now on offer, including precisely those which work through the mechanisms of *pseudo*-involvement.

On the broad question of the interconnectedness which television has brought to perceptions of, and engagement with, national and international issues, it is hard to fault the general indications at work in McLuhan's idea of the 'global village'. After all, a village does not have to be free of tensions, conflicts, and radical inequalities and, in reality, very few are. Yet McLuhan's perception of cultural change is continually disabled by the way in which an interest in sensory connections displaces close attention to social structures and processes. This is nowhere more evident than in the use of the terminology of 'hot' and 'cold' to describe the profile of different media. Television is a 'cool' medium because its communicative profile is low in definition and dispersed across sound and vision, compared to a 'hot' medium like cinema which is visually very strong and highly defined. The attempt to distinguish between 'hot' and 'cool' is flawed by unclear and inconsistently applied criteria, as many critics have noted (see particularly Miller 1972), but the fundamental problem for the concerns of this chapter is the slide from observations about the sensory factors involved in attending to different media to observations about the social consequences of such attendance. A key transitional statement is McLuhan's comment, after remarking on the way in which cool media require data to be 'filled in' by the viewer, reader, or listener, that 'Hot media are, therefore, low in participation, and cool media are high in participation' (McLuhan 1973: 31). It is perhaps open to argument just how much television requires 'perceptual compensation' by the viewer in order to attend to its image, particularly in the context of recent refinements both in image definition, screen size, and sound quality. But it is very much open to argument what this level of perceptual/sensory activity has to do with the cognitive and affective relations between *what* is being shown on the screen and the viewer's mind. In abolishing specific questions of form and content from his account of the televisual experience, McLuhan effectively abolishes all questions of specific social relations too.

Meyrowitz is also interested in the general properties of media as a factor in social change but his perspective is more historically substantive and his primary focus on social (particularly domestic) relations keeps him from the abstracted individualism towards which McLuhan's commentaries regularly drift. He shares in common with many other commentators (notably Ong 1982) the idea that 'electronic media bring back a key aspect of oral societies: simultaneity of action, perception and reaction' (Meyrowitz 1994: 57). In a recent essay which reviews and contextualizes some of the ideas in his major study *No Sense of Place* (1985), he gives an assessment of the impact of electronic media which, whilst it clearly links back to the optimism of McLuhan, also sounds a more critical note;

> As a result of the widespread use of electronic media, there is a greater
> sense of personal involvement with those who would otherwise be
> strangers—or enemies. The seemingly direct experience of distant
> events by average citizens fosters a decline in print-supported notions of
> delegated authority, weakening the power of political parties, unions and
> government bureaucracies. The sharing of experience across nations
> dilutes the power of the nation state.

> While written and printed words emphasize ideas, most electronic media emphasize feeling, appearance, mood. There is a decline in the salience of the straight line—in thinking, in literary narrative, in human-made spaces and organizations. There is a retreat from distant analysis and a dive into emotional and sensory involvement. The major questions are no longer 'Is it true?' 'Is it false?' Instead we more often ask, 'How does it look?' 'How does it feel?' (Meyrowitz 1994: 58)

The earlier part of this comment identifies what is a key element in Meyrowitz's view of electronic culture—the kinds of extended personal involvement which it brings. Strong links with Horton and Wohl's notion of the para-social aspects of broadcasting are evident here (discussed in Chapter 4). It is also worth noting the emphasis which is placed on the extent to which this is in fact a kind of *pseudo*-involvement ('sense of . . .', 'seemingly'). Meyrowitz's work (not unlike Horton and Wohl's in this respect too) seems to be characterized by a strong vein of ambivalence around questions of authenticity in social relations. The second part of the quotation seems far less retrievable for a positive judgement—electronic media encourage a 'retreat' from analysis and a 'dive' into the emotional.

Later in his essay, Meyrowitz speaks more specifically about the implications for knowledge of the changes he charts, again using mixed terms of evaluation:

> Television has lifted many of the old veils of secrecy between children and adults, men and women, and politicians and average citizens. By blurring 'who knows what about whom' and 'who knows what compared to whom', television has fostered the blurring of social identities, socialization stages, and ranks of hierarchy. The electronic society is characterized by more adultlike children and more childlike adults; more career-oriented women and more family-oriented men; and by leaders who act more like the 'person next door', just as average citizens demand to have more of a say in local, national, and international affairs. (Meyrowitz 1994: 68)

Meyrowitz shares with McLuhan, then, the judgement that television has worked against the modes of containment and of hierarchization which previously characterized both knowledge and social relations within print culture. It has encouraged new connections, new empathy, and a new fluidity of boundary between the private and the public. This sounds like the 'good story' about television, a story about the liberation of potential and about a new, richer aesthetics of identity. But within his account, strong elements of a 'bad story' are to be found too. In this story, television skews the relationship between appearance and reality, extending sociality through mechanisms of illusion, and encourages emotional rather than rational engagement, giving up on critical detachment. Meyrowitz seems reluctant to consider the *net* consequence of these various gains and losses, as it bears on the specific kinds of public sphere and private life which television supports. He is also relatively uninterested in the particular industrial and commercial dynamics which have shaped the medium's realization, particularly in North America, and which therefore might be thought to be an important factor in any cultural consequences on the scale his analysis proposes.

A far less ambitious but more convincing defence of television as a tool of knowledge is provided by Paddy Scannell (1989). Drawing on the British experience of public service broadcasting both in radio and television, Scannell takes issue with those who view the development of broadcasting as the cause of a general slide in political and cultural standards:

> To the contrary, I wish to argue for broadcasting in its present form as a public good that has unobtrusively contributed to the democratization of everyday life, in public and private contexts, from its beginning through to today. (Scannell 1989: 136)

His main theme in support of this argument is the extension of 'communicative rights' to an increasing number of the population and the emergence of norms of 'reasonableness' which have encouraged and sustained the development of a culture of democracy:

> I believe that broadcasting has enhanced the reasonable character
> and conduct of twentieth-century life by augmenting claims to
> communicative entitlements. It does this, as I have tried to show,
> through asserting a right of access to public life; through extending its
> universe of discourse and entitling previously excluded voices to be
> heard: through questioning those in power, on behalf of viewers and
> listeners, and trying to get them to answer . . . All this has, I think,
> contributed to new, interactive relationships between public and private
> life which have helped to normalize the former and socialize the latter.
> (Scannell 1989: 161)

He comments on the wide range of hitherto inaccessible events and sources of information made available to the broadcasting audience as well as on the specific achievement of broadcast journalism in setting the terms and conventions (for instance, those of the interview) by which knowledge and debate sustain a mediated democratic polity. There are two features of Scannell's positive claims which might work to qualify their *general* application at the turn of the century. First of all, they constitute a defence of public service broadcasting in a context where the main movement of funding, regulation, and provision, as other chapters in this book attest, is towards a more competitive, commercial, and deregulated system. They celebrate the real achievement of British television in a situation where the old model is being displaced for something much more like the North American model and may, therefore, have increasingly made against it precisely those criticisms which are so familiar from American writing. Secondly, Scannell is also a distinguished historian of radio, and he may be giving undue emphasis to the speech forms of the British broadcasting tradition—to its characteristic modes of address, exposition, and interview and its concern both with expertise and ordinariness. Illuminating though this is, it may underplay the cultural consequences following from the newly intensified circulation of images in public life, a phenomenon which is itself now changing the terms and opportunities for television talk.

Any assessment of the knowledge potential of television, or review of its performance, needs to guard against a narrowness in its focus and in its chosen indicators. I remarked at the start of this chapter that knowledge could be a matter of other than factual programming, with its data, descriptions, propositions, and its model of the reasoning viewer. One of the defining cultural characteristics of television is the very wide variety of ways in which it can offer knowledge. Within this variety, the inferred knowledge which viewers gain from programmes with little or no official knowledge agenda adds up to a vital factor in that centripetal and centrifugal dynamic, the double relationship of cultural ingestion and cultural projection, which I referred to in the introduction to this book. Nor is this kind of knowledge effect necessarily circumstantial. Within fiction particularly, knowledge of human relationships and the diverse conditions of social living are often opened up in a way which is all the more powerful for being carried through an emotional engagement with screened action. Here the resources of dialogue become crucial in portraying an interior life beyond even the most innovative documentary team. For instance, the way in which British soap operas render versions of contemporary, ordinary domestic life and a whole strand of workplace dramas connect with themes around occupation, family, health, money, aspiration, success, and failure, informs social understanding which is as casual as it is deep (on this see, for instance, Brunsdon 1981; Geraghty 1991; Press 1991; D'Acci 1994; Allen 1995). In combination, such portrayals can also help constitute a popular social memory both for contemporary viewers and, differently, for those who view the programmes in later years (Spigel 1995 comments suggestively on this function). Feminist writers have been much more alert to these dimensions of television knowledge than has the mainstream of criticism and research, which has tended to follow the intensive and well-documented debate about the circulation of descriptive and propositional forms. Studies which crossed generic boundaries, and particular the fact/fiction divide, in addressing either substantive areas of social understanding or the forms of knowledge and of knowing themselves, could make valuable progress towards a more comprehensive sense of what television's role in the circulation of contemporary knowledge, 'bad' or 'good', really is.

The Knowledge Profile of Television

In this section, I want to draw together critically some of the strands of commentary about television and knowledge outlined above. I have noted how there is a body of commentary which is primarily concerned with the content of the knowledge made available, commentary which is concerned with the specific forms in which knowledge is presented, and a kind of commentary which works at the more general level of medium–viewer relationships, identifying broader alignments between features of television and shifts in sensory, cognitive, and affective disposition.

Any attempt to assess the knowledge profile of television needs to recognize, if not necessarily reflect, the wider debate about knowledge in postmodern or late-modern society. This debate, in turn, has had as one of its main themes the posing of questions about new ways of collecting, processing, and distributing knowledge. Some of those from whom I have quoted above do, indeed, view television from within a revised framework for approaching questions of knowledge. Others work with a more traditional set of norms. What factors might inform a revised framework?

First of all, recognition has to be made of the vast increase in the amount of information in public circulation. Making this information meaningful as knowledge poses a problem which the French philosopher Jean Baudrillard (1988) regards as a potential, general crisis in the production of public significance. The implications of volume of information for knowledge values are particularly pressing for an international television system moving towards a twenty-four-hour cycle of provision with dedicated information channels. We also know that electronic mediation has introduced new relations of space and time to the production and circulation of knowledge, radically altering the relations between knowledge and place. The social theorist Anthony Giddens (1990) has discussed the ways in which a process of 'disembedding' has 'lifted out' many specialist knowledges from their traditional contexts, allowing for their rearticulation as mass mediated knowledge and their much wider distribution throughout society. But the changes have not been simply to the scale and rate of knowledge circulation, there has also been a shift in the nature of knowledge itself. For instance, the relationships between knowledge and experience have undergone a shift as a result of the disembedding process—knowledge has become more abstractable from experience and aspects of experience have become vicariously available in condensed form. Giddens notes the new levels of 'reflexivity' which have appeared in social knowledge systems, knowledge itself being increasingly knowledge about knowledge, and requiring more frequent update and more complex and extensive systems of inventory. In many spheres, including television and IT, knowledge has become a primary commodity, subject to the variables of market structures in its distributive patterns and its very character and perceived functions.

How does television fit within these changing contexts for knowledge? I think the terms of its visuality and its temporality provide some useful indications here.

■ Visuality

The visual image has strong limitations as a medium of knowledge since it is heavily dependent on the world of appearances and on the physical rather than the abstract. Although the kinds of 'secondary seeing' which television can offer are a powerful source of engagement with the 'look' of the world, its people, things, and settings, and with natural and material process, they do not by themselves possess the capacity for exposition let alone argument. Television's knowledge profile is, in most genres, visually led at the level of representation but is speech led at the level of description and explanation. The drive towards scopic impact and yet the necessity of speech has presented a challenge in the development of factual television genres (news, current affairs, natural history series, art magazines, etc.), many of which have attempted variously to move towards more colloquial address and locate speech within the terms of a personal performance which is also strongly rendered visually (as discussed in Chapter 4).

Television's scopic power is less intense than cinema's, but its range of naturalistic depictions gives its images a reality effect whose psychological appeal some critics have seen to have knowledge-distorting qualities. New formulas for obtaining what is apparently a more direct access to the real are constantly being attempted. In my commentary on this issue in Chapter 3 I looked at how Kevin Robins and Les Levidow (1991) judged the target-video images made available to television during the Gulf War to have turned history into the terms of a video game, thus combining elements of ultrarealism with those of fantasy. It is worth quoting again from their judgements on the specific image-spaces which television created at that time:

> Through the evidential force of the images, we could know about the war, but it was a kind of de-realized war we were knowing. It was at once a way of seeing and a way of not seeing. Drawn into the image, it was as if we were exempted from our responsibility as participants in a reality. (Robins and Levidow 1991: 326)

This raises a number of profound questions about imagery and its effect upon understanding to which I want to return in my concluding comments.

■ **Temporality** Committed to appearances by its need for images, television has little time for reflection. Its durational profile favours concise and pointed speech. The complexity of prose is a risk to comprehension and a disalignment from the image flow will, if sustained for too long, almost certainly lower the level of viewer engagement. Television sustains its double discourse, words and images, *through* time, giving them a rhythm and tempo. Within these terms the viewer (outside of the use of replay facilities with videotaped material) has to see, hear, and follow a textual system across its phases of narrative or expositional development. In Britain, intensified competition is bringing an increase in the tempo of programmes and an adjustment of their internal aesthetic economy, although the various broadcast and narrowcast outlets will take different routes towards optimizing the rhythms and time values of the television they provide for their target viewers (a shift discussed further in Chapter 11). In many applications, television will be primarily developed as a medium of entertainment and diversion, with its knowledge-providing role as a secondary function which has, itself, a requirement to offer the viewer more than accurate information or cogent analysis and argument. Nevertheless, its performance in providing modes of casual, inferred knowledge in its drama, comedy, and entertainment will, if anything, increase in social consequence and will need to be kept fully within the terms of enquiry and debate.

Both the visual and temporal factors of television knowledge can be seen most obviously in the formats and conventions of television news. The domestic political content of news services is in many countries an essential basis for citizenship, providing the integrity of information flow upon which a degree of informed participation can occur. Yet news knowledge is almost by definition narrow and often superficial in character. It is change based and event based. It is committed to surveying a wide news field, allowing little time for sustained development of any one item. Even where not directly determined by picture availability, it is hard for it to sustain coverage for long without an acceptable level of film/video footage. Research (e.g.

Lewis 1985; Goddard *et al.* 1998) has shown some of the comprehension difficulties which viewers experience with news items, quite apart from the very diverse interpretative frameworks they employ in assessing news significance. Its depictions can often be very striking and shocking, although more uncertain in their production of understanding. It is also able to project testimony with far more directness than print journalism. But it is hard for it to achieve the contextual and explanatory depth of much of the best newspaper reporting. In Britain, public service obligations on broadcast news have led to a situation in which it provides, for many viewers, the most serious and extended account of domestic and world events they will receive, given that they either do not take a newspaper or take a popular tabloid whose serious coverage falls well below network news standards. Television journalism is thus vitally positioned in the full spectrum of circulating news knowledge—inadequate in many respects when judged against the reports in élite newspapers but far superior to much popular printed news. Shifts in the nature of news as a television genre, affecting both its terms of selection and presentation (see McManus 1994; Dahlgren 1995) are likely to modify substantially its character as a knowledge source and its role in national knowledge orders.

Vectors of Change

Television has radically altered the scale, speed of circulation, and nature of knowledge in society. It has made most impact in relation to knowledge of public events and public figures and personalities, where its knowledge fields encompass the world of politics and social administration and the world of sports, recreation, and entertainment. Here, its effect has been both to act as a mediator of knowledge and as a new factor in its construction and in its social relations. It has made less impact upon the world of expert knowledges (e.g. specialisms such as the sciences, law, medicine, and the arts disciplines) but it has routinely worked to access lay audiences to bodies of analysis and opinion which they would otherwise find it hard or impossible to comprehend. Here, the development and range of medical programmes and popular science programmes deserve much further attention (see Karpf 1988 and Silverstone 1985 for illuminating and pioneering studies).

The extension of the public knowledge field by television, a process coextensive with television's steady colonization of everyday life (a process noted at points throughout this book), has changed the nature both of public life and private life. I remarked earlier that it has seemed to some not simply to have blurred but to have collapsed the boundaries here. The way in which the backstage areas of public life are now increasingly made visible through television has been widely discussed. The recent television events surrounding the death of Diana, Princess of Wales, provide a notable instance of factors of public distance combining with those of private closeness in a dense and extensive array of mediations. Yet the net increase in visibility which television has brought is still a matter of physical appearances, renderings of surface more than of abstract relations or the interplay of views and opinion. As Thompson (1996) notes, the very terms of the new level of public picturing, of social visualization, offers new opportunities for image management and image control. There is in most television systems a play-off between what Robins and Levidow, in my earlier quotation, describe as that which is screened and that which is 'screened out'. So it is not surprising that assessment of the net effects of television upon public knowledge is difficult. The level of psychological investment in images, the extent to which we are now an image culture, may serve to reduce attention to deficits and imbalances in the real indicativeness and range of the images provided. However, it is by no means clear that viewers are routinely held by the scopic pleasures of television in quite the intense and constraining way that some critics suggest. Levels of disattention and scepticism allow for considerable shifting between kinds of engagement and of accorded credibility and provide scope for viewer self-reflection about what is on the screen in relation to what is already known, believed, and assumed.

In my own assessments, I share with many writers the belief that the possibilities for new and accessible ways of using speech/image combinations for the mediation of knowledge by broadcast television are great. The 'culture of testimony' which is apparent in many new formats is no substitute for analysis but it redresses what has been within many broadcasting systems an inadequate interest in ordinary feelings and too foreclosed a sense of ordinary life.

Opportunities for popular innovation in the treatment of history and science are shown in the success of series both in the United States and Europe, whilst the use of programmes in conjunction with websites has only just begun to be developed and has much to offer imaginative production. The ways in which television's fictions inform our sense of the material and emotional patterns of contemporary living are also far from being a redundant or exhausted part of its communicative capacity and potential.

The computer, through either on-line services or CD-Rom, is quickly becoming a primary domestic resource both for general and expert information, replacing a variety of previous resources for knowledge and pleasure. Compared to television, IT services provide vast amounts of data but are not so developed as media of *interpretation*, thus further opening up the gap between information and knowledge and reconfiguring the patterns of public access to both. Within these patterns, television's level of success in combining popularity with seriousness and in providing for different types of knowing will continue to be a critical feature of modern society and of democratic development.

11

Television 2000: The Terms of Transformation

As I finish this book, television in Britain is fully within a period of radical change, the direction and consequences of which cannot yet confidently be forecast. I remarked in Chapter 2 how some aspects of the change are nationally originated while others are the reflection of international developments. Quite often, national and international factors are combining to create new horizons of policy and new corporate strategies. Only some fifty years old in general application, television has become the world's most significant cultural technology, exerting a profound shaping effect on the nature of everyday modernity. Although its short history has been marked, internationally, by regular technological advances and revisions of its economic and social framing (to regulate its influence, to harness its power, to increase its profitability) it is now possible to see the steady emergence, underneath the local variations, of a new international model and indeed, less directly, a new social and cultural profile for television. This is a model born of many elements, but at the most general infra-structural level it is the combined product of an applied technological development, the new deregulatory energies of the telecommunications market in a global phase of capital accumulation and a hesitancy, in some countries a crisis, in the role of the state as the variously endorsed agency of the public. In essence, the new model takes a technological-given opportunity—expansion and diversification of viewing choice and viewer services—and provides it to consumers within a new regulatory and corporate framework.

The new model is mostly to be found in combination with residual or still dominant elements of national development and is at various stages of ascendancy and rate of advance in different countries. The movement is not towards some final homogeneity (global television, for better or worse) but towards a new and deep level of interconnection and interpenetration across variant national and area systems, affecting some dimensions of television immediately and directly, others more slowly and only through an indirect or rebound process. The new model has a much more aggressively commercial approach than many previous national televisions. Certainly, the British will experience it with more sense of novelty than viewers in North America, but it is not simply the global exportation of an established American system. However, like that system it is grounded in the delivery of television services and programmes as consumer goods for specific sector markets having dynamics both of monopoly and of competition. Some of the services and programmes have a broad transnational character, others are viable with smaller, narrowcast audience groupings. Surrounding and variously integrating with the new model are, of course, the products and experiences offered by the wider revolution in telecommunications and domestic IT. Just what this revised economic and industrial order means for what viewers see on screens, for television's representational and discursive order, is certainly a matter of priority for academic enquiry.

It is possible to see the study of television as caught in a position of double embarrassment in such a situation. It has barely begun to make a full political, social, and cultural assessment of 'television as we know it', yet its very object of study is shifting towards 'television as we knew it' with some speed. However, with such a modest amount of achieved scholarship concerning the ways in which television has changed political, social, and cultural values, it is arguably not very well equipped to engage with 'television as we will know it' or to offer much of a contribution to public debate about the different options (where these exist as a practical reality).

Study of television has often been preoccupied with the contemporary moment, it has been the study of a perpetual present. The limitations of this when, among other things, we now need a steady sense of the past in order to understand the significance of imminent and future change, will quickly become apparent. Being excited by, or apocalyptic about, change is not an adequate response. It is too often accompanied both by a careless relativism about values and by a thin and overly repetitive set of ideas about the promise and threat of 'the global'. Certainly, processes of globalization figure importantly in what is happening to television, but the stratospheric level of many commentaries fails to connect with the articulations of causality and consequence for television as specific and situated industrial systems, creative practices, and cultural experiences. It fails to consider television's significance for real, and different, audiences.

At several points in the preceding chapters, I have referred to the nature and implications of change but in this final chapter I want to reflect on it more directly. In doing so, I shall take aspects of the British situation to provide a point of departure for commentary and a means of illustrating ideas about transformation. Television in Britain is distinctive and many chapters in this book have remarked upon particular features of it. But its current reorganization brings it into complex articulation with television internationally and it is that sense of the international forming the new national that I want to bring out in my discussion. As with my attempts to raise questions of television as an institution in Chapter 2, I also feel it necessary to keep specific substantive circumstances regularly in view, however much the matter of their typicality or generalizability is raised. This is because the shift to an airy transnationalism has too often resulted in work addressing neither the nature of national nor international television but has contributed to the construction of a fiction, an academic object, the 'television' of television studies (on this, see Brunsdon 1997) which often bears little relationship to what is found on the screen or in viewing experience *anywhere*.

This final chapter is also a good opportunity for me to say what further academic developments I would like to see and where I think fresh attention would be welcome. It gives me a chance to pull together the different strands of argument and evaluation in the book and perhaps make more explicit my own sense of it as a project at a particular point in the development both of television and its study.

National within Global: The New Matrix of Television in Britain

There is little doubt but that one consequence of the new television order in Britain will be a dispersal of television's social and cultural identity, paralleling a disaggregation of its productive and distributive structures. What I mean by this is that the proliferation of channels together with the increasing use of television within the context of IT facilities will inevitably reduce the cultural density of television as an element of national life. This density has been the product of a small number of terrestrial channels (initially, the single BBC service) carrying schedules built from the programmes of major institutional producers and holding a very large share of viewing attention. It has been a 'limitation' on television which has allowed the maintenance of a relatively well-defined national profile for the medium—a largely proactive regulatory framework, a high level of shared viewing experience among the population, and a commonly identifiable cultural object for appreciation, criticism, and debate. The imperatives following from the new order will inevitably displace this model, however slowly and whatever the cultural durability which certain elements of traditional television turn out to have.

As in many countries, the introduction of colour (in Britain, during the early 1970s) created a new relation to the cinema, a whole new range of aesthetic recipes for generic development, and (gratifyingly for the trade) the need for viewers to buy or rent new sets. It was, however, the video cassette recorder, increasing in domestic availability throughout the late 1970s and early 1980s, which, rather than simply enhancing established cultural conventions, began to shift the use made of the screen. The rental, and purchase of films, the pre-set recording of material, and the ability to watch one channel and record another all began quietly to modify the specific space/time character of broadcast television and the cultural identity it had maintained in Britain.

The extension of channel choice through cable and satellite continues, although the terms of the play-off between the two systems of distribution (and the degree of dependence of the latter upon the former) are changing. The cabling initiatives undertaken in many parts of Britain by companies offering telephone services are one reason for this, reducing the attractiveness of direct satellite reception. However, we are now entering the era of digital transmission, bringing not only higher picture quality but the possibility of interactivity along with an even wider range of channels than current cabling provides. The phasing of this shift and the development of its full potential, particularly across existing terrestrial channels and proposed new 'pay-per-view' services, will have a profound impact on the ecology of television over the next decade.

The question of how far the television/IT convergence at the level of system will bring about a convergence in the actual *use* of the domestic device has also been much discussed in Britain. As most major audio-visual functions (CD, CD-Rom, telephone, television, internet use, computing applications) become centralizable in one device (see the useful review in Collins and Murroni 1996) it is possible to see single device marketing as the future of the field. However, some recent business forecasts draw attention to the different kinds of domestic space and pattern of use (frequency, time of day, etc.) best suited to these separate functions and predict continuing unit separation as a consumer preference. In these ways, and with national variations, the very instrument of television's domesticity and the core identity of television as a social *object*, is coming under question.

However, while television continues to impact so heavily on national life, both as an agency of information and of entertainment, and on individual imaginative life too, the securing of a responsiveness to the public interest and to public values within the new television order will be a matter of importance, no matter what revision the concept of 'the public' itself undergoes. There is no doubt that this securing will be difficult to achieve. It will be made so by the potential conflict of public value criteria both with private corporate profitability and (even more awkwardly) by the popularity as signalled by the ratings which new kinds of programming may achieve.

As many commentators have noted, that extension of choice which has often been the subject of celebration by the advocates of change deserves closer scrutiny. For whilst it is true that the number of channels available to viewers (within a range of charges) is about to increase radically, the actual increase in *new* product, in newly made sitcoms, documentaries, plays, soaps, etc., is relatively small. A gap between production and distribution is opening up as a result of imminent shifts and many of the new channels will serve largely to repeat material previously shown elsewhere and to give imported (mainly American) material a secondary-market screening. This may not prove an unattractive option but it is far from constituting the cornucopia of boundless televisual inventiveness and creativity conjured up by promoters of change and techno-utopian academics.

It is not surprising, then, that in this context there have been anxieties expressed about the maintenance of quality. As I noted in Chapter 9, quality is a word around which a good deal of recent discussion of television has been generated. Usage of the term as an indicator of cultural value has become conflated both with its more specialized use to register levels of craft skill and its widespread use throughout sectors of industry, now extended to public services, to mean a conformity with objective standards in the interests of product standardization and consumer confidence. Yet despite its consequent proneness to this kind of slippage, it can be seen as an attempt by many of those who use it in good faith to keep issues of cultural value on the agenda in a situation where the movement towards cost-efficiency, preselling, and the optimum targeting of audiences is making such considerations secondary and adjunctive at best.

I have briefly outlined a substantive national situation here, a situation of radical change following on from technological development, corporate restructuring, and a revised and less interventionist regulatory climate. Some countries are much further down the broad trajectory which is implicit in my sketch, others have only begun to negotiate its initial phases, perhaps without any previous, established system to be left behind. Indeed, the difference between national starting-points, even within Europe, is great. What will now be significant are the national differences in the stated social *goals* of change and the national arrangements made for its management. In respect of this outcome, within Europe the interplay between national and transnational institutions, and, everywhere, that between state agencies and market structures, will be decisive. Response to the different kinds of television polity and television culture which are emerging are already modifying, internationally, the agenda and the approach of academic work.

A Changing Agenda of Study

Since the mid-1990s, academic study of television has shown an increased tendency to ponder its own brief history, to audit its gains, and to be more frank about its limitations. At times, a sense of disorientation has shown itself, but such a sense is often the prelude to a more sustained phase of reconstruction. The underdevelopment, fragmentation, and mixture of theoretical uncertainty and assertiveness to be found in the field, as well as changes in the nature of television itself, make such reconstruction necessary.

In this section I want to outline five areas which it seems to me offer a focus for new critical thinking about television, in part developing conceptual strands already established, in part requiring us to produce revised or entirely fresh ideas. These areas are: the terms of the television/IT convergence; the implications of multi-channel choice; the development of historical studies; multi-genre analysis, and international comparisons.

■ Television/IT convergence

What will the new interactivity of television mean for domestic use of the medium? It will certainly bring with it the capacity both for greater purposiveness and selectivity in viewing, reducing, potentially to zero, the role of the schedule in shaping viewing behaviour the more that individualized requests can be met. However, it is unlikely to reduce the casual use of television significantly, even though it increases the intensity and range of purposive use. In the arguments about increasing channel choice, quite apart from an overstatement of choice differences, too much has often been made of the purposive viewing model. In some ways this replicates the emphasis on focused instrumentalism which was a feature of debate about the introduction of home micro-computers in the 1980s and which had then to confront the fact of games-playing as the major domestic use.

In contrast to this, there is the more recent and perhaps much more relevant example of the internet, which in its recreational mode is, classically, 'surfed' in a specific variant of the casual mode of engagement. When the viewer/user is confronted with such an extensive repertoire of choices, spontaneity and fortuitousness (an openness to accident) may become as established a form of leisure usage as purposive search. But interactivity also offers an extension to the televisual not just greater selectivity over its variety. Within this development, programmes potentially lose their self-containedness (contingent though it always is within the flow of the schedule) to become one part of an audio-visual event which is larger and, finally, variably defined by viewer involvement.

We know some of the standard ways in which this involvement is predicted, moving on from the techno-populism of the instant electronic verdict, through the 'which ending to the drama do you prefer?' scenarios, and then into the more intensive authorial modes of electronic dialogue and image exchange. Clearly, the shift from extended and elaborated consumerism (both casual and purposive, in my earlier terms) to the more producerly kinds of application, marks a critical borderline in technology, organization, and cultural usage. Questions of informational availability give way here to questions of aesthetic order, of mode of address, of graphical design, of changed looks and sounds. One pressing requirement, before potential is closed down by imposed 'practicalities', is to debate just what kinds of interactivity *might* extend existing generic formats, in what ways, and for what purposes.

■ **Multi-channel choice**

I have already remarked how the level and kinds of choice which new distribution systems are bringing with them are open to scepticism, a scepticism which may become a factor in determining the real shape of viewing behaviour within those national systems where a radical increase occurs quickly. Regular review of how the overall shift in viewing patterns develops, and then of the emerging pattern for particular groups of viewers, will provide a central project of enquiry in itself and also an informing context for much upcoming reception study. Not only will the plotting of viewers' switchings be of direct interest (see the suggestive pilot study in Jensen 1995) but the new expectations guiding channel selection, the new criteria for viewing, will be of great significance for the future of audio-visual culture. They will link the pleasures and uses of television to wider cultural changes both as cause and as effect. The options for experiencing international programming (increasingly produced as such) will be combined with selective access to the local whilst at the same time there is a redevelopment of both the look and the sound of the national.

What will be the consequences for the generic and aesthetic organization of programmes? I noted earlier in the book how one answer here has to take account of the increased need to hook viewers in quickly and firmly by a programme rhythm (visual, aural, narrativized, performative, presentational, or whatever) which delivers frequent peaks, thereby holding back the finger on the remote control. For many genres, this is likely to be a strong tendency although it is clear that no single recipe for audience retention can be devised, particularly where it is dedicated channels (e.g. those for films and sport) which exert the new pull on what to watch. Whilst it would be silly to underrate the breadth of appeal of action-intensive or strongly exclamatory styles, it is also clear that other, quieter kinds of pleasure are derived from television (as Chapter 9 explored) and that these are likely both to continue and to continue to be profitable.

We can add to this agenda of questions the effects of multi-channelling on production budgets and the way in which the circulation of investment and profit relates to the commodity circulation of the programmes themselves.

In many countries, the newer economy of television is likely to increase radically the gap between the cheap and the expensive end of production, with onward consequences for form, content, and the differentiation of real viewing options and viewing cultures.

■ **Historical studies**

I suggested above that the study of television, like the study of media more generally, has suffered from a lack of historical studies. It has sometimes worked with a frantically contemporary agenda. A comparison can be made with film studies, where, on both sides of the Atlantic, historical enquiries have produced some of the most outstanding scholarship of the last decade. There is a particular problem in Britain, where until recently the emphasis, in such historical work that was undertaken, was heavily on an externalist perspective—privileging questions of policy and organization. Asa Briggs's five-volume history of broadcasting remains the classic account, with a shift to a stronger interest in programmes by volume v (1995), while Scannell and Cardiff (1991) offer a fine cultural history of pre-war radio yet to be paralleled for television. In my own collection (Corner 1991) I brought together work on generic development in the 1950s and 1960s which I thought might mark the start of a phase of historical scholarship on programme culture. As yet, however, only a small number of scholars have developed work within a similar perspective or offered the broader cultural histories of television as an institution to match William Boddy's (1990) account of American network developments in the 1950s. Thumin (1995) offers a useful sketch of what needs to be done in developing both a social history of television as a gendered medium and a sense, however impressionistic and selective, of the historical audience.

Interpreting the present and debating the future are not the only reasons for studying the past, but a firmer sense of the political, social, and cultural relations of the television we have had would help greatly in the reorientation of studies, and the responses to change, which are necessary.

■ **Multi-genre studies**

There have not been enough questions asked about the way in which television representation works across different genres. A quite tightly generic perspective has often been adopted in studies, often in a way which proceeds in ignorance of other kinds of television. This then has implications for the formulation of research questions and the value of answers. The long-standing gap between work on news and work on entertainment is a particular instance of this. One way to go forward might be to look more often at how a specific theme, topic, or event is treated across a range of different genres of output. The primary objective would be to explore the nature of the different transformations performed on pre-televisual material and themes by different production practices and conventions of portrayal. Just how the generic now features in television, the interplay of continuity with innovation, and the relation of form to purpose, would become more sharply available to scrutiny. Such an approach would also encourage a better engagement with the mutual dynamics connecting television's mediations to the broader currents of practical consciousness, of thinking and feeling, active within the culture.

■ **Multi-national comparison** Within a context where a high level of internationalization is apparent and discussion of globalization, in terms of its definition as well as its substantive indicators, is widespread, more studies in comparative analysis are necessary. Comparative historical studies would be particularly valuable in looking at the way in which systems constructed within different frameworks of funding, organization, and policy are modifying in response to technological and corporate shifts at the international level.

Comparative studies offer a challenge for research design if they are to present a fair, sustained comparison developed within a coherence of conceptual scheme and methodological approach. Too often recently, comparative work has been rather careless in this latter respect, linking together diverse studies which share the same broad topic. Two-nation or three-nation studies often offer better opportunities than larger-scale projects since they allow not only for intensive pre-research consultation but also for regular monitoring and adjustment. All aspects of television could benefit from such study but programmes and cultures of viewing have, in the past, been neglected in favour of the more directly institutional issues. A shift here could help develop a richer account of the factors involved in changed global–local relations and in the nature and inter-configuration of subnational, national, and international cultural traits and tendencies (see Straubhaar 1997 on the emerging possibilities and Richardson and Meinhof 1999 for an illuminating comparison of British and German programming).

If these lines of approach were to receive further sustained attention, our knowledge of the social and cultural identity of television and how it is changing internationally would be valuably increased. But throughout this book I have suggested other gaps too (for instance, in production studies, in the double engagement both with interpretation and influence, in the better understanding of television's changing domestic settings) and the according of priorities will inevitably be a matter of some dispute and, in part, a product of the kinds of fit between academic initiative and available funding.

In the introduction to this book I referred to the idea of television as having both centrifugal and centripetal dynamics, ingesting selectively from the wider culture with voracious energy and disseminating images, often with high impetus, across the full range of public and private life. The terms of its influence are notoriously hard to plot with precision but its function in the production of modern identity and consciousness is widely documented and also widely felt. For many years, television has been the principal mediating system of a changing modernity. The dual identity of television as both a knowledge system and a pleasure system, an identity which has been the cause of so many regulatory difficulties and of so much debate about its actual and proper functions, will be maintained through the transformations discussed above and across the continuation of national variants.

I have wanted throughout the preceding chapters to reflect the intellectual vitality surrounding academic discussion of television and the way in which work has drawn both on humanities and social scientific conventions of enquiry. Study of television was always bound to be messy, with speculation and polemic strongly to the fore. The medium's permeation of so many aspects of social life and its depictive diversity, placed under scrutiny by disciplines in theoretical ferment, ensured this.

My stocktaking, in part necessarily historical and also, I am very aware, necessarily selective too (another author would doubtless have drawn up a rather different inventory and given different emphases) has been carried out against a backdrop of fundamental change in the object of study. I have felt it necessary to refer to this backdrop regularly rather than present an account of ideas cut off from substantive systems, practices, and experiences, drawing here on the wider illustrative force of many characteristics of the British television system and the lengthy and wide-ranging debate about its purposes and performance.

Underlying both the approaches to study and substantive change, however, there remain issues which we can be sure twentieth-century television and its analysis will bequeath to those of the twenty-first century. These are issues, at different levels of abstraction and generality, of how market structures variously enhance or impede the continuing project of democracy, of how forms of social solidarity and social inclusion can coexist with individualism, of how commercial profit connects with cultural value, and of how electronic images and recorded speech inform the understanding, excite the imagination, and help form the very nature (for better or worse) of the social and the personal.

References

ABERCROMBIE, N. (1990), 'The Privilege of the Producer', in R. Keat and N. Abercrombie (eds.), *Enterprise Culture* (London: Routledge), 171–85.

ADORNO, T. (1991), *The Culture Industry: Selected Essays on Mass Culture*, ed. J. Bernstein (London: Routledge).

ALLEN, R. (1995) (ed.), *To Be Continued: Soap Opera Around the World* (London: Routledge).

ALTHUSSER, L. (1971), *Lenin and Philosophy and Other Essays* (London: New Left Books).

ALTMAN, R. (1986), 'Television, Sound', in T. Modleski (ed.), *Studies in Entertainment* (Bloomington and Indianapolis, Ind.: Indiana University Press), 39–54.

ALVARADO, M., and BUSCOMBE, E. (1978), *Hazell: The Making of a TV Series* (London: British Film Institute).

ANDERS, G. (1956), 'The Phantom World of TV', *Dissent*, 3: 15–24.

ANDERSON, A. (1997), *Media, Culture and the Environment* (London: University College Press).

ANG, I. (1985), *Watching 'Dallas': Soap Opera and the Melodramatic Imagination* (London: Methuen).

BARKER, M., and PETLEY, J. (1997) (eds.), *Ill Effects* (London: Routledge).

BARTHES, R. (1975), *The Pleasure of the Text* (New York: Hill and Wang).

—— (1977), 'The Rhetoric of the Image', in *Image Music Text*, trans. S. Heath (London: Fontana), 32–51.

BAUDRILLARD, J. (1988), *Selected Writings* (Cambridge: Polity).

BAZIN, A. (1967), 'The Ontology of the Photographic Image', in *What is Cinema?*, i, trans. H. Gray (Berkeley and Los Angeles: University of California Press).

BENJAMIN, W. (1973), *Illuminations* (London: Fontana).

BERNSTEIN, B. (1971), *Class, Codes and Control*, i (London: Routledge).

BODDY, W. (1990), *Fifties Television: The Industry and its Critics* (Urbana, Ill.: University of Illinois Press).

BONDEBJERG, I. (1996), 'Public Discourse/Private Fascination: Hybridization in "True Life-Story" Genres', *Media, Culture and Society*, 18.1: 27–45.

BORDWELL, D., and THOMPSON, K. (1990), *Film Art: An Introduction*, 3rd edn. (New York: McGraw-Hill).

BORN, G. (forthcoming), 'Quality in Television', *Media Culture and Society*.

BRANIGAN, E. (1992), *Narrative Comprehension and Film* (London: Routledge).

BRIGGS, A. (1995), *The History of British Broadcasting in the United Kingdom*, v. *Competition 1955–1974* (Oxford: Oxford University Press).

BROWNE, N. (1984), 'The Political Economy of the TV (Super) Text', *Quarterly Review of Film Studies*, 9: 174–82.

BRUNSDON, C. (1981), '*Crossroads*: Notes on Soap Opera', *Screen*, 22.4: 32–7.

—— (1990), 'Problems with Quality', *Screen*, 31.1: 77–90.

—— (1993), 'Identity in Feminist Television Criticism', *Media, Culture and Society*, 15.2: 309–20.

—— (1995), 'The Role of Soap Operas in the Development of Feminist Television Scholarship', in R. Allen (ed.), *To Be Continued* (London: Routledge), 49–65.

—— (1997), 'What is the "Television" of Television Studies?', in D. Lusted and C. Geraghty (eds.), *The Television Studies Book* (London: Arnold), 95–113.

—— and MORLEY, D. (1978), *Everyday Television: 'Nationwide'* (London: British Film Institute).

BRUNSDON, C., D'ACCI, J., and SPIGEL, L. (1997) (eds.), *Feminist Television Criticism: A Reader* (Oxford: Oxford University Press).

BURGELMAN, J.-C. (1997), 'Issues and Assumptions in Communications Policy and Research in Western Europe', in J. Corner, P. Schlesinger, and R. Silverstone (eds.), *International Media Research* (London: Routledge), 123–53.

BURNS, T. (1969), 'Public Service and Private World', in P. Halmos (ed.), *The Sociology of Mass Media Communicators*, Sociological Review Monograph 13 (Keele: University of Keele), 53–73.

—— (1977), *The BBC: Public Institution and Private World* (London: Macmillan).

CALDWELL, J. T. (1995), *Televisuality* (New Brunswick, NJ: Rutgers University Press).

CAMPBELL, C. (1995), *Race, Myth and the News* (London: Sage).

CARROLL, N. (1996), *Theorizing the Moving Image* (Cambridge: Cambridge University Press).

CAUGHIE, J. (1991a), 'Adorno's Reproach: Repetition, Difference and Television', *Screen*, 32.2: 127–53.

—— (1991b), 'Before the Golden Age: Early Television Drama', in J. Corner (ed.), *Popular Television in Britain: Studies in Cultural History* (London: British Film Institute), 22–41.

COLLINS, R., and MURRONI, C. (1996), *New Media, New Policies* (Cambridge: Polity).

CORNER, J. (1980), 'Codes and Cultural Analysis', in *Media, Culture and Society*, 2.1: 73–86.

—— (1991) (ed.), *Popular Television in Britain* (London: British Film Institute).

—— (1995), *Television Form and Public Address* (London: Arnold).

—— (1996a), *The Art of Record* (Manchester: Manchester University Press).

—— (1996b), 'Reappraising Reception: Aims, Concepts and Methods', in J. Curran and M. Gurevitch (eds.), *Mass Media and Society*, 2nd edn. (London: Arnold), 280–304.

—— (1996c) (ed.), *Media, Culture and Society*, 18.1 (issue theme: 'Changing Forms of Actuality').

—— (1997), 'Television in Theory', *Media, Culture and Society*, 19.2: 247–62.

—— RICHARDSON, K., and FENTON, N. (1990), *Nuclear Reactions: Form and Response in Public Issue Television* (London: John Libbey).

—— HARVEY, S., and LURY, K. (1994), 'Culture, Quality and Choice: The Re-Regulation of ITV 1989–91', in S. Hood (ed.), *Behind the Screens* (London: Lawrence and Wishart), 1–19.

COTTLE, S. (1995), 'The Production of News Formats', *Media, Culture and Society*, 17.2: 275–91.

D'ACCI, J. (1994), *Defining Women: Television and the Case of Cagney and Lacey* (Chapel Hill, NC: University of North Carolina Press).

DAHLGREN, P. (1995), *Television and the Public Sphere* (London: Sage).

DANIELS, T. (1997), 'Television Studies and Race', in D. Lusted and C. Geraghty (eds.), *The Television Studies Book* (London: Arnold), 131–40.

DAVIDSON, M. (1991), *The Consumerist Manifesto* (London: Routledge).

DAYAN, D., and KATZ, E. (1992), *Media Events* (Cambridge, Mass.: Harvard University Press).

DIENST, M. (1994), *Still Life in Real Time* (Durham, NC: Duke University Press).

DOWNING, J. (1996), *Internationalizing Media Theory* (London: Sage).

EAGLETON, T. (1983), *Literary Theory* (Oxford: Blackwell).

ECO, U. (1972), 'Towards a Semiotic Enquiry into the Television Message' (translated from the 1965 Italian original), *Working Papers in Cultural Studies*, 3 (Birmingham: University of Birmingham), 102–31.

ELLIOTT, P. (1972), *The Making of a Television Series* (London: Constable).

—— (1974), 'Uses and Gratifications Research: A Critique and a Sociological Alternative', in J. Blumler and E. Katz (eds.), *The Uses of Mass Communication: Current Perspectives for Gratification Research* (Beverley Hills: Sage), 249–68.

ELLIS, J. (1982), *Visible Fictions* (London: Routledge).

ERICSON, R., BARANEK, P., and CHAN, J. (1987), *Vizualizing Deviance* (Milton Keynes: Open University Press).

FAIRCLOUGH, N. (1995), *Media Discourse* (London: Arnold).

FEUER, J. (1983), 'The Concept of "Live Television": Ontology as Ideology', in E. A. Kaplan (ed.), *Regarding Television* (Los Angeles: American Film Institute/University Publications of America), 12–22.

—— KERR, P., and VAHIMAGI, T. (1984), *MTM: Quality Television* (London: British Film Institute).

FISH, S. (1980), *Is There a Text in This Class?* (Cambridge, Mass.: Harvard University Press).

FISKE, J. (1987), *Television Culture* (London: Methuen).

—— (1991), 'Postmodernism and Television', in J. Curran and M. Gurevitch (eds.), *Mass Media and Society* (London: Arnold), 55–67.

—— and HARTLEY, J. (1978), *Reading Television* (London: Methuen).

FORNAS, J. (1995), *Cultural Theory and Late Modernity* (London: Sage).

FRANKLIN, B. (1994), *Packaging Politics* (London: Arnold).

FRASER, N. (1990), 'Rethinking the Public Sphere: A Contribution to the Critique of Actually Existing Democracy', *Social Text*, 25/26: 56–80.

FRITH, S. (1983), 'The Pleasures of the Hearth: The Making of BBC Light Entertainment', in *Formations* editorial collective (eds.), *Formations of Pleasure* (London: Routledge), 101–23.

GARNHAM, N. (1990), *Capitalism and Communication: Global Culture and the Economics of Information* (London: Sage).

—— (1995), 'Comments on John Keane's "Structural Transformations of the Public Sphere"', *The Communication Review*, 1.1: 23–5.

—— (1996), 'Constraints on Multimedia Convergence', in W. Dutton (ed.), *Information and Communication Technologies* (Oxford: Oxford University Press), 103–19.

GAVIN, N. (1998) (ed.), *Media, Economy and Public Knowledge* (London: Cassell).

GERAGHTY, C. (1991), *Women and Soap Opera* (Cambridge: Polity).

GIDDENS, A. (1990), *Modernity and Self-Identity* (Cambridge: Polity).

GILLESPIE, M. (1995), *Television, Ethnicity and Cultural Change* (London: Routledge).

GITLIN, T. (1983), *Inside Primetime* (New York: Pantheon).

GODDARD, P., *et al.* (1998), 'Television Economic News and the Dynamics of Public Response', in N. Gavin (ed.), *Media, Economy and Public Knowledge* (London: Cassell).

GOFFMAN, E. (1959), *The Presentation of Self in Everyday Life* (New York: Doubleday Anchor)

GOLDIE, G. W. (1977), *Facing the Nation: Television and Politics, 1936–76* (London: Bodley Head).

GOLDMAN, R. (1992), *Reading Ads Socially* (London and New York: Routledge).

GRAMSCI, A. (1971), *Selections From The Prison Notebooks*, ed. Quintin Hoare and Geoffrey Nowell-Smith (London: Lawrence and Wishart).

GRAY, A. (1992), *Video Playtime* (London: Routledge).

GRAY, J. (1995), *Enlightenment's Wake: Politics and Culture at the Close of the Modern Age* (Oxford: Oxford University Press).

GREIMAS, A. J. (1966), *Semantique structurale* (Paris: Larousse).

GRIPSRUD, J. (1995), *The 'Dynasty' Years: Hollywood Television and Critical Media Studies* (London: Routledge).

—— (1997), 'Television, Broadcasting, Flow: Key Metaphors in TV Theory', in D. Lusted and C. Geraghty (eds.), *The Television Studies Book* (London: Arnold), 17–32.

HABERMAS, J. (1989), *The Structural Transformation of the Public Sphere* (Cambridge: Polity).

HALL, S. (1973), 'Encoding and Decoding in the Television Discourse', CCCS Stencilled Paper 7 (Birmingham: University of Birmingham Centre for Contemporary Cultural Studies).

HALL, S. (1977), 'Culture, the Media and the "Ideological Effect"', in J. Curran, M. Gurevitch, and J. Woollacott (eds.), *Mass Communication and Society* (London: Arnold), 315–48.

—— (1994), 'Reflections upon the Encoding/Decoding Model: An Interview with Stuart Hall', in J. Cruz and J. Lewis (eds.), *Viewing, Reading, Listening* (Oxford: Westview), 253–74.

—— CRITCHER, C., JEFFERSON, T., CLARKE, J., and ROBERTS, B. (1978), *Policing the Crisis: Mugging, the State and Law and Order* (London: British Film Institute/Open University Press).

HARVEY, S. (1994), 'Channel 4 Television: From Annan to Grade', in J. Corner and S. Harvey (eds.), *Television Times* (London: Arnold), 102–29.

HEATH, S. (1990), 'Representing Television', in P. Mellencamp (ed.), *Logics of Television* (Bloomington, Ind.: Indiana University Press), 267–302.

—— and SKIRROW, G. (1977), 'Television: A World in Action', *Screen*, 18.2: 7–59.

—— —— (1986), 'An Interview with Raymond Williams', in T. Modleski (ed.), *Studies in Entertainment* (Bloomington, Ind.: Indiana University Press), 3–17.

HEIDE, M. (1995), *Television, Culture and Women's Lives* (Philadelphia: University of Pennsylvania Press).

HERMAN, E., and MCCHESNEY, R. W. (1997), *The Global Media* (London: Cassell).

HILL, A. (1997), *Violent Entertainment* (Luton: John Libbey).

HORTON, D., and WOHL, R. (1956), 'Mass Communication as Para-Social Interaction: Observations on Intimacy at a Distance', *Psychiatry*, 19: 215–29. Reprinted in J. Corner and J. Hawthorn (1993) (eds.), *Communication Studies*, 4th edn. (London: Arnold), 156–64.

HUSBAND, C. (1994) (ed.), *A Richer Vision* (London: John Libbey/UNESCO).

INNIS, H. (1951), *The Bias of Communication* (Toronto: University of Toronto Press).

ISER, W. (1978), *The Act of Reading* (Baltimore: Johns Hopkins Press).

JENSEN, K. B. (1986), *Making Sense of the News* (Aarhus: The University Press).

—— (1995), *The Social Semiotics of Mass Communication* (London: Sage).

—— (1996), 'The Empire's Last Stand: Reply to Rosengren', *European Journal of Communication*, 11.2: 261–7.

JHALLY, S., and LEWIS, J. (1992), *Enlightened Racism: Audiences, 'The Cosby Show' and the Myth of the American Dream* (Boulder, Col.: Westview Press).

KARPF, A. (1988), *Doctoring the Media: The Reporting of Health and Medicine* (London: Routledge).

KATZ, E., and LAZARSFELD, P. (1955), *Personal Influence* (New York: Free Press).

—— BLUMLER, J., and GUREVITCH, M. (1974), 'Utilization of Mass Communications by the Individual', in J. Blumler and E. Katz (eds.), *The Uses of Mass Communication* (London: Faber), 19–32.

KEANE, J. (1991), *The Media and Democracy* (London: Polity).

—— (1995), 'Structural Transformations of the Public Sphere', *The Communications Review*, 1.1: 1–22.

KILBORN, J. (1994), 'How Real Can You Get?: Recent Developments in Reality Television', *European Journal of Communication*, 9.4: 421–39.

—— (1996), 'New Contexts for Documentary Production in Britain', *Media, Culture and Society*, 18.1: 141–50.

KOZLOFF, S. (1992), 'Narrative Theory and Television', in R. Allen (ed.), *Channels of Discourse, Reassembled* (London: Routledge), 67–100.

LANG, K., and LANG, G. (1953), 'The Unique Perspective of Television', in *American Sociological Review*, 18.1: 3–12. Reprinted in J. Corner and J. Hawthorn (1993) (eds.), *Communication Studies*, 4th edn. (London: Arnold), 187–97.

LEISS, W., KLINE, S., and JHALLY, S. (1986), *Social Communication in Advertising* (London: Methuen).

LEWIS, J. (1985), 'Decoding Television News', in P. Drummond and R. Paterson (eds.), *Television in Transition* (London: British Film Institute).

—— (1991), *The Ideological Octopus: Explorations into the Television Audience* (New York and London: Routledge).

—— (1997), 'What Counts in Cultural Studies?', *Media, Culture and Society*, 19.1: 83–97.

LIVINGSTONE, S., and LUNT, P. (1994), *Talk on Television* (London: Routledge).

LLOYD, S. (1951), 'Minority Report' to the Report of the Committee on Broadcasting 1949 (Cmnd 8116) (London: HMSO), 201–10.

LULL, J. (1991), *China Watches* (London: Routledge).

LURY, K. (forthcoming), *Cynicism and Enchantment* (Oxford: Oxford University Press).

LUSTED, D., and GERAGHTY, C. (1997) (eds.), *The Television Studies Book* (London: Arnold).

MACARTHUR, C. (1975), '*Days of Hope*', *Screen*, 16.4: 139–44.

MACCABE, C. (1974), 'Realism and the Cinema: Notes on Some Brechtian Theses', *Screen*, 15.2: 7–27.

—— (1976), '*Days of Hope*: A Response to Colin McArthur', *Screen*, 17.1: 98–101.

MCGREGOR, B. (1997), *Live, Direct and Biased?* (London: Arnold).

MCLAUGHLIN, L. (1993), 'Feminism, the Public Sphere, Media and Democracy', *Media, Culture and Society*, 15.4: 599–620.

MCLUHAN, M. (1964), *Understanding Media* (London: Routledge and Kegan Paul; page references from Abacus edn., London, 1973).

MACMANUS, J (1994), *Market-Driven Journalism* (Thousand Oaks, Calif.: Sage).

MCNAIR, B. (1996), *Mediated Sex* (London: Arnold).

MCQUAIL, D. (1994), *Mass Communication Theory: An Introduction* (Newbury Park, Calif.: Sage).

MANDER, J. (1978), *Four Arguments for the Elimination of Television* (Brighton: Harvester Press).

MASCIAROTTE, G.-J. (1991), 'C'mon Girl: Oprah Winfrey and the Discourse of Feminine Talk', *Genders*, 11.1: 81–110.

MESSARIS, P. (1994), *Visual Literacy: Image, Mind, and Reality* (Boulder, Col.: Westview).

MEYROWITZ, J. (1985), *No Sense of Place: The Impact of Electronic Media on Social Behaviour* (New York: Oxford University Press).

—— (1994), 'Medium Theory', in D. Crowley and D. Mitchell (eds.), *Communication Theory Today* (Cambridge: Polity), 50–77.

MILLER, D., and PHILO, G. (1996), 'The Media Do Influence Us', *Sight and Sound*, December: 18–20.

MILLER, J. (1972), *McLuhan*, Modern Masters Series (London: Fontana).

MILLER, M. K. (1987), 'Prime Time: Deride and Conquer', in T. Gitlin (ed.), *Watching Television* (New York: Pantheon). Text citations from republication in M. Alvarado and J. O. Thompson (1990) (eds.), *The Media Reader* (London: British Film Institute), 295–320.

MILLINGTON, B., and NELSON, R. (1986), '*Boys From the Blackstuff*': The Making of TV Drama* (London: Comedia).

MODLESKI, T. (1982), *Loving With a Vengeance: Mass Produced Fantasies for Women* (London: Methuen).

MOORES, S. (1993), *Interpreting Audiences* (London: Sage).

—— (1996), *Satellite Television and Everyday Life* (Luton: John Libbey).

MORLEY, D. (1974), 'Reconceptualising the Media Audience', CCCS Stencilled Paper 9 (Birmingham: University of Birmingham Centre for Contemporary Cultural Studies).

—— (1980), *The 'Nationwide' Audience* (London: British Film Institute).

—— (1981), 'The Nationwide Audience: A Critical Postscript', *Screen Education*, 39: 3–14.

—— (1986), *Family Television* (London: Routledge (Comedia)).

—— (1995), 'Television: Not So Much a Visual Medium, More a Visual Object', in C. Jenks (ed.), *Visual Culture* (London: Routledge), 170–89.

MORRISON, D. (1992), *Television and the Gulf War* (London: John Libbey).

MORSE, M. (1985), 'Talk, Talk, Talk', *Screen*, 26.2: 2–15.

MOSCO, V. (1996), *The Political Economy of Communication* (London: Sage).

MULGAN, G. (1990) (ed.), *Questions of Quality* (London: British Film Institute).

MUMFORD, L. S. (1997), 'Feminist Theory and Television', in D. Lusted and C. Geraghty (eds.), *The Television Studies Book* (London: Arnold), 114–30.

MURDOCH, R. (1989), MacTaggart Lecture delivered at the Edinburgh International Festival, 25 Aug. 1989.

MURDOCK, G. (1993), 'Communication and the Constitution of Modernity', *Media, Culture and Society*, 15.4: 521–39.

NEGUS, K., and DU GAY, P. (1994), 'The Changing Sites of Sound: Music Retailing and the Composition of Consumers', *Media, Culture and Society*, 16.3: 395–413.

NELSON, R. (1996), 'From *Twin Peaks*, USA, to Lesser Peaks, UK', *Media, Culture and Society*, 18.4: 677–82.

NICHOLS, B. (1991), *Representing Reality* (Bloomington, Ind.: Indiana University Press).

—— (1994), *Blurred Boundaries* (Bloomington, Ind.: Indiana University Press).

ONG, W. (1982), *Oracy and Literacy: The Technologizing of the Word* (London: Methuen).

O'SULLIVAN, T. (1991), 'Television Memories and Cultures of Viewing, 1950–65', in J. Corner (ed.), *Popular Television in Britain* (London: British Film Institute), 159–81.

PARKIN, F. (1972), *Class, Inequality and Political Order* (London: Paladin).

PATERSON, R. (1980), 'Planning the Family: The Art of the Television Schedule', *Screen Education*, 35: 79–85.

PETERS, J. D. (1993), 'Distrust of Representation: Habermas on the Public Sphere', *Media, Culture and Society*, 15.4: 541–71.

PHILO, G. (1990), *Seeing and Believing* (London: Routledge).

POSTMAN, N. (1986), *Amusing Ourselves to Death* (London: Methuen).

PRESS, A. (1991), *Women Watching Television* (Philadelphia: University of Pennsylvania Press).

RADWAY, J. (1984), *Reading the Romance: Women, Patriarchy and Popular Literature* (Chapel Hill, NC: University of North Carolina Press).

RICHARDSON, K., and CORNER, J. (1986), 'Reading Reception: Transparency and Mediation in Viewers' Accounts of a TV Programme', *Media, Culture and Society*, 8.4: 485–508.

—— and MEINHOF, U. (1999), *Worlds in Common?* (London: Routledge).

RIDELL, S. (1996), 'Resistance Through Routines', *European Journal of Communication*, 11.4: 557–82.

ROBINS, K., and LEVIDOW, L. (1991), 'The Eye of the Storm: Reviewing the Gulf War', *Screen*, 32.3: 324–8.

ROSENGREN, K. E. (1996), Review article of K. B. Jensen's *The Social Semiotics of Mass Communication*, *European Journal of Communication*, 11.1: 129–41.

ROSS, A. (1989), *No Respect: Intellectuals and Popular Culture* (London: Routledge).

ROSS, K. (1996), *Black and White Media* (Cambridge: Polity).

SCANNELL, P. (1989), 'Public Service Broadcasting and Modern Public Life', *Media, Culture and Society*, 11.2: 134–66.

—— (1991) (ed.), *Broadcast Talk* (London: Sage).

—— (1996), *Radio, Television and Modern Life* (Oxford: Blackwell).

—— and CARDIFF, D. (1991), *A Social History of British Broadcasting*, 1 (Oxford: Blackwell).

SCHLESINGER, P. (1978), *Putting 'Reality' Together* (London: Constable).

—— (1990), 'Rethinking the Sociology of Journalism', in M. Ferguson (ed.), *Public Communication: The New Imperatives* (London: Sage), 61–83.

—— MURDOCK, G., and ELLIOTT, P. (1983), *Televising 'Terrorism': Political Violence in Popular Culture* (London: Comedia).

—— DOBASH, R. E., DOBASH, R. P., and WEAVER, C. (1992), *Women Viewing Violence* (London: British Film Institute).

—— and TUMBER, H. (1994), *Reporting Crime: The Media Politics of Criminal Justice* (Oxford: Oxford University Press).

SCHRODER, K. (1992), 'Cultural Quality: Search for a Phantom?', in K. Schroder and M. Skovmand (eds.), *Media Cultures* (London: Routledge).

SCHUDSON, M. (1995), *The Power of News* (Cambridge, Mass.: Harvard University Press).

—— (1996), 'The Sociology of News Revisited', in J. Curran and M. Gurevitch (eds.), *Mass Media and Society*, 2nd edn. (London: Arnold), 141–59.

SHATTUC, J. (1997), ' "Go Ricki": Politics, Perversion and Pleasure in the 1990s', in D. Lusted and C. Geraghty (eds.), *The Television Studies Book* (London: Arnold), 212–25.

SILVERSTONE, R. (1981), *The Message of Television: Myth and Narrative in Contemporary Culture* (London: Heinemann).

—— (1985), *Framing Science: The Making of a BBC Documentary* (London: British Film Institute).

—— (1994), *Television and Everyday Life* (London: Routledge).

SMYTHE, D. W. (1954), 'Reality as Presented by Television', *Public Opinion Quarterly*, 18.2: 143–56.

SPARKS, C. (1998), *Television and Democracy in Eastern Europe* (London: Sage).

SPIGEL, L. (1992), *Make Room for Television* (Chicago: University of Chicago Press).

—— (1995), 'From the Dark Ages to the Golden Age: Women's Memories and TV Re-Reruns', *Screen*, 36.1: 16–33.

STRAUBHAAR, J. (1977), 'Distinguishing the Global, Regional and National Levels of World Television', in A. Sreberny-Mohammadi, D. Winseck, J. McKenna, and O. Boyd-Barrett (eds.), *Media in a Global Context* (London: Arnold).

THOMPSON, J. (1990), *Ideology and Modern Culture* (Cambridge: Polity).

—— (1995), *The Media and Modernity* (Cambridge: Polity).

THUMIN, J. (1995), 'A Live Commercial for Icing Sugar', *Screen*, 36.1: 48–55.

TODOROV, T. (1977), *The Poetics of Prose* (Oxford: Blackwell).

TULSON, A. (1985), 'Anecdotal Television', *Screen*, 26.2: 60–4

TULLOCH, J., and ALVARADO, M. (1983), *Doctor Who: The Unfolding Text* (London: Macmillan).

TUNSTALL, J. (1993), *Television Producers* (London: Routledge).

WERNICK, A. (1991), *Promotional Culture* (London: Sage).

WHITE, D. M. (1950), 'The Gatekeeper: A Case Study in the Selection of News', *Journalism Quarterly*, 27.4: 383–90.

WILLIAMS, R. (1960), 'Advertising: The Magic System', *New Left Review*, 4: 27–32.

—— (1962), *Communications* (Harmondsworth: Penguin).

—— (1974a), *Television: Technology and Cultural Form* (London: Fontana).

—— (1974b), 'Drama in a Dramatized Society', Inaugural Lecture, Faculty of English, University of Cambridge. Reprinted in A. O'Connor (1989) (ed.), *Raymond Williams on Television* (London: Routledge), 3–13.

WILLIAMSON, J. (1978), *Decoding Advertisements* (London: Marion Boyars).

WINSTON, B. (1995), *Claiming the Real* (London: British Film Institute).

Index